In a time where the church feels just as fractured as our nation, we need Christians who are equipped and compelled to repair the breach. In this book, Dominique Gilliard calls us back to biblical discipleship and shows the scriptural roots of some of the most divisive issues that impair our witness—privilege, systemic oppression, and racial justice. *Subversive Witness* is a gift to the church, offering us a new, faithful way forward amid the brokenness and polarity that abounds.

—**Latasha Morrison**, founder of Be the Bridge to Racial Unity, author of the New York Times bestselling book *Be the Bridge: God's Heart for Racial Reconciliation*

In this historic moment, many are asking, "What can I do?" With the passion of a community advocate and the inspirational teaching gifts of a seasoned pastor, Dominique Gilliard reimagines the biblical narratives of familiar characters such as Esther, Moses, and Paul to demonstrate how privilege can be generative and liberating, compelling us to participate as ambassadors of God's justice in innovative and subversive ways.

—**Robert Chao Romero**, author of *Brown Church: Five Centuries of Latina/o Social Justice, Theology, and Identity*

Subversive Witness rightly highlights the connections between privilege and power. No matter what your social-cultural location, this book compels us to recognize the various forms of power we possess— oftentimes unjustly—and what we can do to bring about equity and justice. Those readers who have humble hearts to walk through the confession, lamentation, and repentance that this book encourages will cultivate a witness that can shake the world.

—**Jemar Tisby**, CEO of The Witness, Inc.

Dominique Dubois Gilliard reminds us about our proximity to privilege in *Subversive Witness* and how we as Christians are tasked to handle, recognize, and ultimately steward that privilege to bring heaven on earth. This is an important and timely message that needs to be internalized by the church and faith-professing individuals alike.

—**Albert Tate**, cofounder and lead pastor of Fellowship Church, Monrovia, CA

How should Christians engage a world with systems and structures that are so often unjust, racist, and prevent human flourishing? How can Christians overcome their addictions to comfort and apathy to leverage their power and privilege for those in need of God's liberating work? If these are real questions for you—and they should be—Dominique Gilliard leads us forward in offering robust answers through an absolutely persuasive reading of the Christian Scriptures. Gilliard shows us how the stories of Moses, Esther, Paul and Silas, and Jesus should form the church to be a people patterned after the character of Jesus, who used his power and privilege for the good of those most in need. I can't wait to use this book as required reading in my own courses!

—**Joshua W. Jipp**, associate professor of New
Testament, Trinity Evangelical Divinity School

In *Subversive Witness*, Dominique Dubois Gilliard offers the scriptural context that is so often missing from the conversation around privilege. With the critical reflection of a biblical scholar, the piercing proclamation of a prophet, and the deep compassion of a pastor, Gilliard methodically and carefully asks his reader to reimagine a radically discipled misunderstanding of repentance, power and privilege.

Gilliard's timely and thoughtful analysis boldly calls us to overthrow the systematized mythology and ahistorical (often whitewashed) theology that "privatized" privilege often fosters—vying instead for the living out of a Christianity which is authentically grounded in the gospel of the Lord Jesus Christ and well positioned to subversively *wield privilege* as a revolutionary tool for creating a more equitable society where all persons can flourish.

For all who care deeply about the witness of the American church, this book is a must read. It is, quite simply, the best book on Christian ethics I have read in some time.

—**Rev. Cecilia J. Williams**, president and CEO of the Christian
Community Development Association (CCDA)

This book is an absolute gift that can shake us out of our discontent and help each of us navigate a turbulent and troubled world to bring healing and wholeness to our communities and world. Dominique Gilliard not only offers a brilliant critique of what true repentance is all about but also offers us a way forward in how to use our privilege to usher in justice for our neighbors. He dives deep into the Scriptures, offering us much-needed and often-overlooked context to understand the challenges and choices some of our most revered biblical characters faced, reminding us that the challenges we face today are nothing new. But in the process, he offers us a new way of thinking about privilege and how to wield it to bring heaven to earth. At a time when the church has often taken a back seat in the face of so much injustice, I can't think of a better or more timely book to help each of us navigate and ultimately use who we are to subvert the status quo and bring about God's kingdom here on earth.

—**Jenny Yang,** vice president for advocacy and policy, World Relief

Subversive Witness initiates a long-overdue discussion within the church on power and privilege and the ways these have been deformed by empire. Far from taking the familiar approach of disavowing privilege, Gilliard instead calls Christians to leverage privilege for the sake of exposing oppression and tackling injustice. He offers a spectacular accounting of Scripture's hope for collective liberation without curtailing its cost. As an academic dean and Christian ethicist, I hope to see this book as required reading in seminaries, churches, and theological institutions across the world!

—**Michelle Clifton-Soderstrom,** dean of faculty,
North Park Theological Seminary

With the myriad of challenges facing the church today, we need the prophetic call to go deeper—deeper into our faith and deeper into the biblical narrative. Dominique Gilliard has offered a gift to the American church by calling out our assumptions around the confoundingly contentious use of the word *privilege*. Our witness as a racially reconciled Christian community requires us to examine our failure as witnesses to the truth of the gospel because of our failure to deal with truth. Through this text, Gilliard calls us into a deeper discipleship that takes us further into God's word so that we may find the healing balm of truth. May the reader take heed and act upon these important words.

—**Soong-Chan Rah**, Robert Munger Professor of Evangelism, Fuller Theological Seminary, author of *The Next Evangelicalism* and *Prophetic Lament*

Dominique Gilliard has given us a gift! As a pastor, I'm regularly in conversation with people around matters of privilege. So much gets lost in the conversation because there isn't a comprehensive theological framework that guides our engagement with each other. This is why I'm so grateful for this book. Gilliard has given us an accessible, nuanced, prophetic resource to help us name the power and privilege we possess and leverage it for the good of others and the glory of God.

—**Rich Villodas**, lead pastor of New Life Fellowship, author of *The Deeply Formed Life*

Truly a book for these days. *Subversive Witness* gives a scriptural, historical, and hard-hitting way forward through the current divisive talk. Healing and hope at the highest level. Discipleship at its best! This should be a resource for every believer in Jesus.

—**Jo Anne Lyon**, general superintendent emerita, the Wesleyan Church

Like in the singular *Rethinking Incarceration*, Dominique Gilliard doesn't just point something out; he points the way. *Subversive Witness* is not just a solution but a sign. It highlights our blind spots as the church and illustrates how racism hides in systems, how we can advance the kingdom, and how to address systemic problems. This is essential reading for the times in which we live.

—**Gregory Boyle**, founder of Homeboy Industries, author of *Tattoos on the Heart*

SUBVERSIVE WITNESS

SUBVERSIVE WITNESS

SCRIPTURE'S CALL TO LEVERAGE PRIVILEGE

DOMINIQUE DUBOIS GILLIARD

ZONDERVAN
REFLECTIVE

ZONDERVAN REFLECTIVE

Subversive Witness
Copyright © 2021 by Dominique DuBois Gilliard

Requests for information should be addressed to:
Zondervan, *3900 Sparks Dr. SE, Grand Rapids, Michigan 49546*

Zondervan titles may be purchased in bulk for educational, business, fundraising, or sales promotional use. For information, please email SpecialMarkets@Zondervan.com.

ISBN 978-0-310-12403-0 (hardcover)
ISBN 978-0-310-12404-7 (ebook)
ISBN 978-0-310-12405-4 (audio)

Cover design: Micah Kandros Design
Interior Design: Sara Colley

Printed in the United States of America

21 22 23 24 25 26 27 28 29 30 /LSC/ 14 13 12 11 10 9 8 7 6 5 4 3 2 1

To parents who sacrificed, struggled, and persevered more than I will ever fully understand to provide me with the opportunities I have been blessed with.

To my son, Turé, whom I love more than life itself. I vow to relentlessly toil to make this world a better place for you to grow up in.

To the descendants of the Greenwood District of Tulsa, Oklahoma, who lost loved ones in the desecration of Black Wall Street one hundred years ago. On the centennial of this travesty, I dedicate this book to you, lamenting that the sin of white supremacy robbed you of your ancestors and demolished the most prosperous Black community in US history.

Over the span of two days, enraged white citizens, who envied the success of Black business leaders, burned the flourishing community of the Greenwood District of Tulsa, Oklahoma, to the ground, decimating thirty-five city blocks filled with Black businesses, homes, and churches. One hundred fifty Black businesses and 1,265 homes were destroyed. Three hundred Black people were killed, eight hundred more were injured, and nine thousand were left homeless. The white mob caused $1.8 million in damages, which equates to roughly $25 million in today's dollars. The community has never truly recovered, and it has taken the Oklahoma school system a century to construct a curriculum in which students from elementary through high school learn about this catastrophe.

This tragedy should be included—in age appropriate ways—in history textbooks nationwide and should be recorded as either the "Greenwood Massacre" or the "desecration of Black Wall Street," not as the Tulsa Race Riots. It is because of the grave price this community, and others like it, paid that I am able to bear witness today.

CONTENTS

Foreword by Mark Labberton xiii

Introduction xvii

1. Understanding Privilege and Its Power 1
2. Pharaoh's Daughter: Leveraging Privilege to
   Resist Systemic Sin 21
3. Esther: Leveraging Privilege to Stand in Solidarity 39
4. Moses: Leveraging Privilege to Birth Liberation 61
5. Paul and Silas: Leveraging Privilege to Create
   Systemic Change 83
6. Jesus: Abandoning and Leveraging Privilege to
   Proclaim the Good News 97
7. Zacchaeus: Leveraging Privilege to Foster Social
   Transformation 119
8. Scripture's Call to Repentance 151
9. Producing Fruit in Keeping with Repentance 169

Acknowledgments 189
Notes 191

FOREWORD

I was born into privilege.

Now if that conjures a silver spoon, it's not what I mean. I was raised in a third-generation immigrant's home in a middle- to lower-middle-class family in a moderate-sized agricultural town in the middle of Washington State. We primarily lived in modest, rented homes. My dad's intellectual energy was driven by science and innovation; he studied engineering for three years, though he did not finish his degree. My mom's education concluded in the twelfth grade.

Was I privileged? Astoundingly so. I had an intact, loving family with no addictions, no violence, no fear. My parents fed my brother, Kurt, and me healthy food during our nightly dinners together and cooked us breakfast every morning. They believed in us and cheered us on. My brother and I could dare to take risks and were thrilled when many of them paid off. We found success and access far beyond our social rank.

Kurt and I were school athletes. We didn't struggle with underlying health or developmental conditions. We were born male, which spared us many residual sexist limitations and opened doors that undoubtedly made some things much easier for us than for girls of our ages. We were good students, challenged by dedicated public school teachers who cared for and inspired us. And we had close, meaningful, and longstanding friendships with each other and within our neighborhood and school.

What's more, we were white in a largely white town, within and around which were the Yakima Nation and a substantial number of itinerant, seasonal Latino farm workers. Our parents supported us through college, and while my brother went to the Naval Academy—in part to save my parents the financial burden of tuition—my folks sacrificially supported my private undergraduate education.

Privilege. Thick privilege. The list could go on, including things like my seminary and graduate education, my remarkable and loving wife, my two priceless sons, and my unexpected appointment as a faculty member and then president of my own esteemed seminary. My point is not to show off but to acknowledge these privileges honestly and candidly. Compared to most people, life has been stacked in my favor. For years, many of these privileges were invisible to me—another mark of privilege. Once they became apparent, I tried to remain conscious of all these benefits. But awareness, even gratitude, is not enough.

Years ago, when I was a very new Christian, I was alone on a long and familiar mountain drive. I began to feel intensely aware of the gifts I had received by that point in my life, especially when weighed alongside the national and global racial, gender, and economic inequities in much of the world. "Why," I wondered, "was I given so much? What am I to do with such privilege?"

In my heart, I hoped the answer would be to live more

gratefully. Instead, the Spirit said, "Give away what you have received. That is why it was given to you." That road trip changed my life.

Living as a privileged disciple is primary to kingdom life, but it is difficult. God is still dismantling and repurposing the privilege in my life. I'm encouraged by the witness of Christian friends—men and women of varied races, ethnicities, and nationalities from different generations—who every day quietly get on with self-offering and unselfish love. I pray for many of them daily, in part because I must continue to learn from them how to reorient my life to follow Christ.

For years, I only read one email on Sunday mornings before I went to preach. It was a weekly update from two friends serving in a context of extreme poverty and need in Asia. That email was a glorious and anguished portrait of their reality, their story of leveraging privilege. If the life I lived and the gospel I preached only fit a privileged world like mine and not theirs, I should just be silent. If my sermon didn't move us toward offering our privilege for the sake of others, I should quit. And if the congregation didn't engage such a gospel, we should shutter the doors, sell the property, and give it all away. On more than a few Sundays, I went home convicted, if not indicted.

Each of us participates in a world of disordered power, personal and systemic. It's everywhere, and none of us are free from being its perpetrators or victims—and frequently we are both. But what do those of us with thick privilege do with it? Guilt may or may not be relevant, but how do we hold, deploy, or sacrifice what is ours for the justice and thriving of others?

We have to weigh our privilege, sparing none of it from critical examination—repenting when our privilege is blind to its origins, presumptions, and abuses, and offering thanks when our privilege can be given away freely and without coercion. Privilege is not neutral. God hears the cries of the poor and sacrificed his life to change the narrative. His followers—privileged disciples—are to be part of that new story.

That is Dominique Gilliard's urgent cry in this valuable book. Why, where, and how can privilege be poured out such that God's loving and just reign can be seen and tasted in a world that so desperately needs it? How can Christians with privilege serve as a subversive witness to the not-yet of Christ's reign, creating a more just and equitable world?

To be clear, these are not questions for armchair reflection. Nor are they about easing guilt or stoking it. Every day, privileged readers of this book can choose to move beyond our comfort, complacency, or passivity to urgent deference to and empowerment of those on the brutal receiving-end of privilege. In the midst of dismantling the injustices and abuses of privilege, how can it be deployed through the good use of power to undo and redo the bad uses of power?

Underneath and woven through Gilliard's masterful exposition and appeal, I sense a self-controlled scream. He lays out a logical and compelling argument for privileged Christian people to reorder power, even as he is motivated by the protracted cries of suffering, pain, and injustice of those whose voices are not even heard, let alone trusted.

"To whom much is given, much will be required," said Jesus. Herein lies God's freedom and joy for all. This is to be our subversive witness.

MARK LABBERTON
President, Fuller Theological Seminary

INTRODUCTION

I wrote this book to animate the stagnant faith of discontent sisters and brothers who yearn to see and pursue the coming of the kingdom on earth as it is in heaven. I pray it revives the faith of those who have walked away from God, as well as those considering walking away, and transforms the witness of believers who are well adjusted to the unjust status quo. *Subversive Witness* seeks to name, address, and deconstruct the spiritual strongholds arresting the church and distorting our witness. It aims to illuminate that God's Word is truly a lamp for our feet and a light on our path. This book reframes the narratives of key biblical characters to demonstrate their relevance today and to show how their faithfulness is constructive for our ethics and pursuit of life together as one interconnected body.

This book traces Scripture's call to repent—what provokes it, how we heed it, and why repentance transforms us. It specifically explores John the Baptist's timeless call to "produce fruit in keeping with repentance" (Matt. 3:8). Conversely, it also details the consequences of unrepentant sin, hard-heartedness, and living in denial.

The church has largely failed to heed John the Baptist's call, chiefly because we have diluted how the Bible defines repentance. Rather than an actual turning away from sin to return to God and reestablish right(eous) relationship with our Creator, neighbors, and creation, within too many congregations repentance is defined and practiced as merely oral confession. Due to this, many Christians do not understand the difference between apologizing and repenting. This domesticated, unbiblical understanding of repentance bears no fruit and lacks the power to transform broken people, relationships, systems, and structures.

Our lack of repentance conforms us to the patterns of this world, keeping us content amid sinful inequities and complicit with systemic sin and injustice. We have become well adjusted to things to which our faith calls us to be diametrically opposed. Privilege, for example, is a social consequence of our unwillingness to name, turn from, and address sin. The church should lead the way in naming oppression, confessing our role in it, and addressing as well as eradicating the systemic disparities privilege engenders. However, conversations about privilege in the church generally end in one of three places: churches and members deny that privilege exists, consider the topic too controversial to address, or lament feeling immobilized by its weight. This book elucidates that the gospel offers us another way! Acts 6:1–7 offers a clear illustration of this.

Seeing Privilege, Addressing Discrimination, and Sharing Power

As Acts 6 opens, the disciples believed they were functioning as a healthy, missional, interconnected body of Christ. They were actively making disciples, fulfilling the Great Commission, and welcoming new members into God's family. However, they were oblivious to the injustice happening along the margins of their community, to the discrimination in their midst.

In accordance with God's character, we who are God's people are called to sacrificially love our neighbors, particularly to care for the most vulnerable. Throughout the Old Testament, Israel did this via gleaning laws[1] and practicing Jubilee.[2] In Acts 6 the disciples sustained this tradition by instituting a food distribution program for vulnerable widows. A challenge ensued, however; the food program served widows of two different cultural backgrounds, and those two groups of widows had divergent experiences within the program.

The Hebraic widows were cultural insiders with direct access to the city and church's dominant culture, customs, and language. The Hellenistic widows were Jews who lived most of their lives in Greek-speaking cities and towns outside of Jerusalem and returned to the city as cultural outsiders. The Hellenist widows felt as if their outsider status was causing them to be overlooked and marginalized in the church's distribution of food.

The Hebraic widows had advocates at the table of power, as well as cultural, linguistic, and relational advantages that led to them receiving superior treatment. They had privilege. Meanwhile, the Hellenistic widows lacked representation at the decision-making table and were without an advocate in leadership who saw their suffering and identified with their marginalized experience.

Consequently, the church did not care for Hellenistic widows with the same care, intentionality, and love as it did for

Hebraic widows. The exclusively Hebraic leadership had a blind spot, and the distribution disparity went unacknowledged until Hellenistic Jews brought a formal complaint. This matter was one of the earliest challenges the church faced as it started becoming multicultural.

Once the complaint was raised, the disciples assessed the institutional structure and program. They demonstrated their maturity in Christ through their response to the complaint. Instead of being defensive, denying the problem, or trying to cover it up, the disciples conducted a sober assessment of the program and determined that the discrimination claim was legitimate. They did not try to explain away the problem or cast the Hellenistic widows as being divisive for raising the complaint. Not only did the church's leadership acknowledge there was a problem, but they also confirmed that it was systemic. Then they took proactive steps to address it.

To ensure the discrimination problem did not recur, church leadership called a communal meeting and collectively discerned how to address it. They determined there was a need for a council to oversee the food distribution program. The disciples tasked the community with selecting seven men who were known to be full of the Spirit and wise to oversee the program. The overwhelmingly Hebraic community met and selected seven men—Stephen, Philip, Procorus, Nicanor, Timon, Parmenas, and Nicolas—who were all Hellenist. These seven leaders resolved the problem and became an ecclesial model for confronting privilege, addressing discrimination, and sharing power.

As a result of the church's maturity, verse 7 explains, "The word of God spread. The number of disciples in Jerusalem increased rapidly, and a large number of priests became obedient to the faith." The church's willingness to confront privilege and address discrimination led to the spread of the gospel in Jerusalem and beyond. The newly constructed Jerusalem Council, led by Hellenists, became a crucial bridge that expanded the kingdom, enabling the gospel to reach the gentile world. Acts traces this progression "from Cyprus and Cyrene" going north to Antioch, where members of the council were the first to preach the gospel directly to non-Jewish Greeks (11:19–21).[3] This is a beautiful story illustrating why we must humbly respond to discrimination complaints, address privilege in our midst, and equally prioritize the Great Commission and the Greatest Commandment—we are called to fulfill both, not just one or the other.

Liberation and Participation

Instead of denying that privilege exists, sidestepping the topic, or feeling overwhelmed by its weight, the gospel demonstrates how we should deal with privilege. Scripture affirms that privilege is real and declares that while we have the option to exploit it for selfish gain or passively benefit from it, we are called to acknowledge and faithfully steward it. We are called to leverage privilege to further the kingdom and love our neighbor. This book explains how we can do this, and it does so by looking carefully at privileged biblical characters who used what God entrusted to them to bear a subversive witness. The following chapters outline how these biblical characters' faithful witness serves as a practical model for our modern context. They also spell out how privilege can become a subversive tool employed to help usher in the kingdom of God in unique ways.

This book reframes how we read and interpret Scripture. It challenges readers to identify and remove the storybook frames we learned to see biblical characters through. It reveals how privilege can hinder us from perceiving and responding to God's call on our lives. But it also demonstrates how privilege can be generative and liberating, compelling us to participate as ambassadors of reconciliation in innovative and subversive ways. The Spirit of God will not abandon us when we step out in faith and bear our cross daily; Scripture assures us that our labor for the Lord is not in vain.

Privilege has a multitude of expressions. Think about the witness of an often-overlooked biblical character: Lydia (see Acts 16:11–15, 40). She was a woman of privilege, a wealthy businesswoman who understood that she was blessed by God to be a blessing to others. Lydia recognized that God had not entrusted her with wealth to hoard her resources or to construct a buffer between her and the pain and suffering of her neighbors.

Lydia understood that her resources were to be used to make God's name known and love shown. She is renowned for her stewardship, how she used her fortune to further the kingdom and love her neighbors. Lydia offered her home to provide refuge for those oppressed by systemic injustice, and her home was the first gathering place for Christians in Philippi, commonly called the city's first Christian church.

Lydia saw her privilege as something emboldening her to participate in the kingdom through serving those in need. How we use what God has entrusted us with is a powerful testimony to those around us, and Lydia leveraged her privilege to demonstrate to the world who and whose she was.

Privilege, however, does not mean that someone has not

endured trials and tribulations. Scripture reveals that God also entrusts people who have endured oppression with privilege. After enduring abuse and being sold into slavery by his brothers, Joseph was liberated by God, who then entrusted him with privilege (see Gen. 37–47). Joseph became vizier, the second most powerful position in Egypt.

If Joseph's heart had not been in the right place, he would have abused his power and privilege to enact revenge against his brothers. However, God kept Joseph's righteous anger from spiraling into bitterness, and when given the opportunity to return evil for evil, Joseph chose to show God's love, ultimately remembering that his privilege had a missional purpose. Joseph bestowed unmerited grace upon his brothers, loving them in the same manner that God first loved us.

God calls privileged people to strategically leverage our access, influence, and resources to subvert the status quo and advance the kingdom. Our possessions are not just for us; they are things we are called to steward to further the kingdom and sacrificially love our neighbors. God does not entrust people with privilege to exploit it for selfish gain; privilege is supposed to be used to bear a subversive witness, to usher in the inbreaking kingdom and participate in the *missio Dei*. However, as fallible people, we are prone to allowing privilege to control us instead of allowing the Spirit to guide our steps and stewardship of privilege.

Racism, patriarchy, classism, and other forms of privilege— and the -isms that produce these privileges—are not of God. They are not a part of God's original intent. They are not power dynamics God condones, and they are not patterns to which Christians should conform. We are called to pattern our lives after Jesus, our crucified and resurrected Savior.

The disparities that flow from these *isms* are a consequence of sin, our institutionalization of it, and unwillingness to repent of it. Nevertheless, it is undeniable that God entrusts people with privilege and power, with a missional purpose of creating life, flourishing, and fostering shalom[4] where death, destruction, and oppression have reigned for far too long.

What to Expect in This Book

This book invites readers to see faithfulness to God as resistance against the death, theft, and destruction Satan seeks to induce. In a world marred by sin, division, and injustice, the church seeks the kingdom first, on earth as it is in heaven, by choosing sacrificial love in the face of fear, hatred, and indifference. Where apathy abounds, we are afforded an opportunity to bear witness to who and whose we are by choosing cruciform (reflective of the self-giving love displayed for us by Jesus on the cross) solidarity. As we demonstrate that we are Jesus' disciples by our love for one another, empowered by the Spirit, we have an opportunity to fulfill the Great Commission and the Greatest Commandment, immensely expanding the kingdom.

This book reckons with power and privilege. It explores institutional and individual power. It connects power to status, access, and endowment. It aims to help readers understand that how we choose to wield power matters because it bears witness to our principles, priorities, and values. *Subversive Witness* seeks to inspire readers to reimagine how we think about, see, and exercise power, particularly the power of the people, but most specifically the power of God's people who are empowered by the Holy Spirit. This book explores the correlation between power and privilege, and homes in on how privilege should be understood and leveraged by followers of Jesus.

Chapter 1 defines privilege, explains how it was conceived, and what sustains it. It illuminates how Satan uses privilege to distort the truth, revise history, and prohibit us from acknowledging sin and moving toward repentance. This chapter concludes by explaining how Scripture highlights privilege and gives us tools to move beyond denying its existence and feeling incapacitated by it. The good news is that Scripture offers us a blueprint for how we can subversively leverage privilege to further the kingdom and sacrificially love our neighbors.

The second chapter shows how privilege manifests within worldly empires. It then shifts from focusing on tyrannical leadership to emphasizing how the apathy and complicity of constituents emboldens oppressors and grants despotic leaders the legitimacy they need to lead. The chapter then breaks down the content of Exodus 1:6–22 and 2:1–10 to reveal how God's daughters subversively used their vocation, status, and privilege to further the kingdom and love their vulnerable neighbors.

Chapter 3 explores how Esther became queen and unearths the damage we do theologically when we gloss over the circumstances that gave rise to her reign. It then details her experience in the palace and the temptations she overcame to faithfully respond to God's call on her life. The chapter concludes by showing how God reconnected Esther to the pain of her people and compelled her to subversively use her influence and power to save them.

Chapter 4 traces the life of Moses. It begins by looking at the identity crisis that emerged out of being a Hebrew raised in Pharaoh's house. It then unpacks how trauma impacted

Moses' life and impeded his ability to recognize and respond to God's call for a season. Moses did not always get it right, and he did not always realize who he was or what he was called to. He spent many years indulging his privilege, but the Spirit of God disrupted his contentment and led him into the wilderness where he rediscovered who he was created to be. The chapter concludes by outlining how Moses forsook the luxuries of the palace to participate in the kingdom.

Chapter 5 unpacks Acts 16 to illustrate how Paul and Silas used the privilege and power citizenship imbued to unmask a corrupt criminal justice system and hold it accountable. It explains their countercultural choice to refuse to exploit their privilege to opt out of suffering. Instead of using privilege to avoid persecution, the gospel compelled them to choose cruciform solidarity to bring about change. Their witness becomes a model for privileged Christians regarding how to leverage privilege to expose oppression, hold unjust systems and structures publicly accountable, and love vulnerable neighbors. This chapter presses us to consider how we enter into cruciform suffering with our neighbors who do not have the privilege of opting out and then calls us to discern how we can subversively leverage our privilege to create needed systemic change today.

Chapter 6 shows how Jesus epitomizes why it is necessary at times to abandon privilege. He also demonstrates that while privilege is something we can exploit for self-gain, those who faithfully follow him will commit to stewarding privilege by putting the needs of others before their own. Privilege thereby becomes a means to seek the peace and prosperity of our cities, because the counterintuitive kingdom truth is that this is where our individual flourishing is also found. We do not thrive in our pursuit of selfish ambition but in self-giving, sacrificial love, which we only know because Christ first extended it to us.

Jesus also illustrates how God's love compels us to go into places and spaces we would never choose on our own. However, empowered by the Holy Spirit, we do so to bear witness to our mission in the inbreaking kingdom of God by intentionally leveraging our privilege in ways that proclaim good news to the poor, birth liberation for the captive (both those captive to the immobilizing weight of privilege and those held captive in systems and structures of injustice due to it), and give sight to the blind (those who continue to deny privilege exists and those who cannot see God's liberating action due to their suffering amid injustice).

The seventh chapter explains the oppression that made tax collecting such a lucrative vocation. It then breaks down the story of Zacchaeus, the chief tax collector who got rich by extorting his neighbors. The chapter moves to describe his radical transformation upon encountering Jesus. Zacchaeus's repentance is a model for us regarding how we produce fruit in keeping with repentance and leverage privilege for justice. The chapter concludes by exploring contemporary expressions of reparations.

Chapter 8 explores some of the things we need to repent of and outlines what Scripture says about repentance. It then presents spiritual practices that engender repentance as well as illustrates how the love of God liberates us to abide by John the Baptist's call to bear fruit in keeping with repentance.

Unchecked privilege distorts our vision and prevents us from seeing that we are inherently connected to one another. It leads us to think in us-versus-them ways that are antithetical to the kingdom. The last chapter casts a new vision of belonging, one that challenges us to understand privilege not as something that divides us but as a tool to employ to engender social transformation and deeper kingdom participation. Scripture explains that the world will know that we are Christ's disciples by our love for one another. Few things distort this love like unbridled privilege. However, a proper understanding of our call to steward privilege empowers us to bear witness to God's love in innovative, surprising, and sacrificial ways that allow us to expand the kingdom, love our neighbor, and produce fruit in keeping with repentance.

CHAPTER 1

UNDERSTANDING PRIVILEGE AND ITS POWER

I lead an immersive discipleship experience called Sankofa. This racial justice pilgrimage connects the civil rights movement to today's fight for freedom. We sojourn to sacred places where my ancestors' blood cries out from the ground. We explore the robust history of domestic terrorism, systemic racism, and institutional sin, and then unpack the church's complicity. Some of our pilgrimage destinations include a home that was part of the Underground Railroad; the 16th Street Baptist Church in Birmingham, Alabama, where four Black little girls were killed on a Sunday morning by a bomb planted at the base of the church's sanctuary; and the Edmund Pettus Bridge, in Selma, Alabama, the site of Bloody Sunday, where on March 7, 1965, state troopers assaulted and brutalized nonviolent protesters advocating for Black voting rights.[1] This march was led by civil rights icons like Diane Nash, Prathia Hall,

Amelia Boynton (who invited Martin Luther King Jr. to come to Selma), Dr. Martin Luther King Jr., Hosea Williams, and the late congressman John Lewis, who had his skull fractured by officers instigating violence during this peaceful protest.

The Edmund Pettus Bridge, however, is not just significant because of the brutality of Bloody Sunday. The bridge is important because of its location and contentious name. Edmund Pettus is regarded as a hero by many Alabamians. He was a lawyer, decorated general in the Confederate Army, and US senator for eleven years. Alabama historian Wayne Flynt describes Pettus as a man who grew up and lived "in an area full of people who oppose secession. He is going against the grain. He's not a reluctant pragmatist, brought to secession to go along with the people. He's a true believer."[2] In the months prior to the Civil War, Pettus encouraged his older brother, John, who was the governor of Mississippi, to have the state leave the Union and join the Confederacy. Pettus's ardent support of white supremacy gave rise to his political career and climaxed with him being appointed the Grand Dragon of the Alabama Klan—its highest-ranking official.

The Edmund Pettus Bridge was constructed over the Alabama River, a vitally important route for Alabama's slave economy. The bridge was dedicated to Pettus in 1940, thirty-three years after his death. Naming the bridge after Pettus was not just an act of veneration memorializing a Civil War hero; it was an intentional act of violence intended to further the Lost Cause myth and remind Black people of their subordinate place.

Selma is and has been a mostly Black city, and Flynt says naming the bridge after Pettus was a "sort of in-your-face reminder of who runs this place."[3] Flynt says Selma "would've been a place where place names [like the name of this prominent bridge] were about [Black people's] degradation."[4] John Giggie, a history professor at the University of Alabama, affirms Flynt's conclusion, explaining, "The bridge was named for him, in part, to memorialize his history, of restraining and imprisoning African-Americans in their quest for freedom after the Civil War."[5]

Flynt explains that even if Pettus never enacted violence himself, "there's really no way of excluding Edmund Pettus of responsibility from the violence. He helps organize it, he helps protect it, and he does not seek to prosecute anyone who did it."[6] And Giggie writes, "Pettus became for Alabama's white citizens in the decades after the Civil War, a living testament to the power of whites to sculpt a society modeled after slave society."[7]

The fact that someone with this immoral legacy has had a monument standing in his honor for more than eighty years illuminates the indelible link between privilege and power. Those with privilege have the authority to tell, alter, and erase history. Privilege affords those who possess it the ability to recast narratives, nations, and false gods in their own image. While I firmly believe that no person should be forever defined by their worst deed, I also know that the Bible calls us to confess, lament over, and repent of our sins.

At an event honoring John Lewis in Alabama, Caroline Randall Williams, a direct descendent of Pettus, said,

> We name things after honorable Americans to commemorate their legacies. That bridge is named after a treasonous American who cultivated and prospered from systems of

degradation and oppression before and after the Civil War. We need to rename the bridge because we need to honor an American hero, a man who made that bridge a place worth remembering. John Lewis secured that bridge's place on the right side of history. We are not a people that were made to cling to relics of the past at the cost of our hope for the future. Renaming the bridge in John Lewis's honor would be a testament to the capacity for progress, the right-mindedness and striving toward freedom that are at the heart of what's best about the American spirit.[8]

Unchecked, privilege fosters mythology, emboldening an ahistorical theology and worldview. It allows whitewashed history to be canonized and institutionalized, immoral men to be venerated and revered, and nations to live in denial and unrepentant sin. Bryan Stevenson, the executive director of the Equal Justice Initiative, explains how this has played out in the US.

In Rwanda, no one who comes there is allowed to spend time there without hearing about the genocide. In Germany, there is a commitment to remind people about the pain and suffering of the Holocaust. In the United States, it is the opposite. Not only are we not committed to telling [the] truth about slavery, lynching, and segregation, we have actually erected an iconography about a false story: how grand and glorious the 19th century was; how honorable the architects and defenders of slavery were; how fantastic it was to live in the first half of the 20th century; and how noble these elected leaders were while preaching segregation forever, or war.[9]

Unbridled privilege emboldens immaturity, trivializes oppression, and derails our pursuit of shalom. When we are not honest about what divides us, reconciliation becomes a facade for sustaining the status quo, and the body of Christ becomes a place where "Peace, peace," is proclaimed when there is no peace.

Stevenson expounds on the relationship between truth and reconciliation.

> I think we all want reconciliation. We want peace, we want understanding, we want redemption—all of these wonderful things. But we haven't committed ourselves to truth-telling. Truth and reconciliation are not simultaneous. They are sequential. Tell the truth first, and it's the truth that motivates you to understand what it will take to recover, repair, endure—to reconcile.[10]

The body of Christ is called to be a signpost of God's love, mercy, and justice in the world. We cannot fulfill this calling if we continue to live in denial and unrepentant sin. We need truth to live into our created purpose and to move forward together.

Jesus said in John 8:32, "The truth will set you free." Truth empowers the church to establish a common memory and helps us realize how we have conformed to the patterns of this world. Georges Erasmus, a First Nations leader from Canada, explained why establishing a common memory is so important. He said, "Where common memory is lacking, where people do not share in the same past, there can be no real community. Where community is to be formed, common memory must be created."[11] As a covenant people, memory roots us in God's promises, prompts us to remember God's sovereignty, and reminds us of our identity in Christ. We were created for a purpose: to worship God, making our Creator's name known and love shown throughout the world; fulfilling the Great Commission and the Greatest Commandment.

Legislative, Economic, and Educational Privilege

Privilege comes in many forms, and not every manifestation holds the same social currency. In the United States, race, gender, citizenship, class, education, sexual orientation, and able-bodiedness have been the chief expressions of privilege, with race, gender, citizenship, and class historically holding the most weight. Privilege is also stackable, meaning a person can possess multiple privileges at once. For example, initially only free, landowning, white men could be US citizens. Individuals who possessed five privileges—status (freedom), class, race, gender, and citizenship—were politically valued and socioeconomically subsidized over and against all others. That means that from its inception the US gave wealthy white men access to property, power, resources, and wealth that all other people were denied for nearly 144 years.

Moreover, after this period of exclusive access, white people were democratically endowed with unique access to important resources until at least 1965. This unique access has endowed most white children with the privilege of growing up in secure neighborhoods with premium amenities, matriculating in superior schools, and having access to more lucrative vocational opportunities. It has also included a criminal justice system that has legislated with a white bias. The vestiges of this history of systemic injustice linger and continue to undermine our proclamation of "liberty and justice for all."

For example, school funding in the US derives from three sources. While the percentages vary from state to state, generally 45 percent of a local school's funding comes from local property taxes, 45 percent comes from state funding, and 10 percent comes from federal funding.[12] Property values vary immensely from neighborhood to neighborhood and district to district. With that variance come vacillating tax revenues. These economic disparities create inequalities regarding access to quality education nationwide. Consequently, since the early 1970s, nearly every state has seen at least one lawsuit concerning school funding and equity.

A recent study examined the 13,000 traditional public school districts in the US and found about 7,600 where more than 75 percent of students were white and about 1,200 where more than 75 percent of students were nonwhite. While the nonwhite school districts were much larger (usually located in large cities) than the white districts, the two groups had nearly the same number of students: 12.8 million children in nonwhite districts and 12.5 million in white districts.[13]

However, in 2016 nonwhite districts received nearly $54 billion in local tax dollars—or about $4,500 per student—while white school districts, which had higher incomes and lower poverty rates, collected more than $77 billion—or just over $7,000 per student.[14] On average, states added another $6,900 per student to white districts and almost $7,200 per student in nonwhite districts. The comprehensive gap in state and local funding was $23 billion. White districts, on average, had more than $2,000 more in funding per student than nonwhite districts.[15]

The report found the following:

> Despite more than a half-century of integration efforts, the majority of America's school children still attend racially concentrated school systems. This is reflective of the long history of segregation—policies related to everything from voting to housing—that have drawn lines and divided our communities.
>
> Race and class are inextricably linked in the U.S. When comparing the poverty level of racially concentrated systems, a clear divide emerges. Predominantly white districts are far better off than their heavily nonwhite peers. These statistics confirm what we know about income inequality and the effects of segregation.
>
> In the United States, 20% of students are enrolled in districts that are both poor and nonwhite,[16] but just 5% of students live in white districts that are equally financially challenged.[17]

This is only one example of how white students have continued to enjoy unique access post–1965. This unique access continues to order society.

How Privilege Shapes Society

We will never learn to leverage privilege to further the kingdom and love our neighbors if we continue to deny the existence of privilege. Acknowledging privilege is not about condemnation, shaming, or guilting one another into coerced actions. Christians are called to acknowledge privilege because it is real and because doing so liberates us from its power. Confronting and addressing privilege liberates us to live into our created purpose fully and freely.

Acknowledging privilege should not be contentious. Privilege exists because of our unwillingness to deal soberly with structural sin and the legacy of inequity it has bred. Fundamentally, privilege is the by-product of our ancestors' sins and the rotten fruit of the church's indifference to systemic oppression and complicity with evil. Privilege is rarely neutral or benign; it almost always comes at the expense of our neighbors.

Privilege connected to embodiment (how our bodies are constructed—race, gender, health, and more) slowly but surely negates the fundamental biblical truth that we all are made equally in the image of God. It therefore subtly creates a sliding scale of humanity, where some lives are respected, protected, and valued over and against others. Privilege is the offspring of hardened hearts and unrepentant spirits. It shrewdly sustains and frequently expands systemic injustice, social inequities, and targeted oppression. Privilege is not just something certain individuals are endowed with; it also becomes institutionalized, perverting a society's customs, education, laws, and practices.

Many people possess privilege and experience marginality concurrently. White women, for instance, because of white supremacy and their proximity to white men, have been granted privileges and access that people of color have largely been denied. For example, of the $120 billion worth of new housing subsidized by the government between 1934 and 1962, less than 2 percent went to nonwhite families.[18] People of color were locked out of home ownership, while white Americans were essentially given exclusive access. Nevertheless, the racial privilege white women enjoyed did not negate the sexism and patriarchy they were subjected to. White women, while enjoying racial privilege, were still denied the full rights of citizenship and democratic participation until 1920—144 years after white men but 45 years before most people of color.

Similarly, men of color benefit from male privilege but are excluded from the perks of whiteness. We do not have to overcome sexism and patriarchy—in fact, we benefit from them—but we are relentlessly hounded by racism. We have a categorically different experience than white men.

Just as privilege is stackable, so is oppression. Women of color, particularly undocumented, uneducated, impoverished, and/or disabled women of color, uniquely elucidate this. Legal scholar Kimberlé Crenshaw coined the term *intersectionality* to describe this phenomenon, the overlapping oppression that women of color endure.[19] These women must overcome systemic barriers that others do not, and our inability, or perhaps more precisely, unwillingness to acknowledge this, is rooted in sin.

Possessing privilege does not mean your life is necessarily easy. Nor does it mean you have not endured hardships. It does, however, mean that if you struggled to overcome, you had fewer barriers to clear—particularly systemically and legislatively— than you would have had without your privilege. As a person with privilege, this may seem insignificant. If it does, know that the obstacles you are minimizing and brushing off have thwarted your neighbor's pursuit of progress, equity, and justice for centuries. For instance, the federal government, under the Home Mortgage Disclosure Act, revealed in 2004 that when people of color are approved for mortgages, they are more likely to receive higher cost "subprime" loans. These loans are offered at rates that are 0.1 percent to 0.6 percent higher than its standard rates. While this difference may seem inconsequential, over time it equates to thousands of dollars in additional interest payments. Interest on a thirty-year, $180,000 mortgage loan at a 6.5 percent interest rate would total about $21,000 more than the same mortgage loan at a 6 percent rate.[20] Privilege blinds its beneficiaries to the many unjust policies like this that still exist and allows them to minimize how profoundly these injustices continue to shape society.

Looking Out for Our Own

Privileged people also benefit from having most people in positions of power see them as relatable and identifiable. Psychologically, this is known as ingroup bias, the tendency to favor our own group above others.[21] Research demonstrates that this bias leads people in power to treat those within their group(s) with more compassion, civility, dignity, and empathy.[22] The selective compassion and empathy that ingroup bias engenders makes a mockery of justice. From *Dred Scott* to Betty Shelby, from the Fugitive Slave Act to the Fair Sentencing Act, we have witnessed how ingroup bias has repeatedly aborted justice and bred legal malpractice.

Our nation's tragic history of legislative discrimination sets a lamentable precedent for judges who continue to allow ingroup bias to pervert their verdicts. For example, in 2015 Aaron Persky—a white judge—sentenced Brock Turner—a white drunken college student from a wealthy family who sexually assaulted an unconscious woman—to six months in jail and probation. Persky defended his historically lenient sentence by saying anything more than this would have a "severe impact" on Turner's bright future.[23]

Another white judge, Jean Hudson Boyd, sentenced the white, sixteen-year-old Ethan Couch, who killed four people while driving under the influence, to less than two years in jail. During the case, Boyd validated a ludicrous affluenza argument rendered by Couch's lawyers, which epitomized privilege. Couch's defense successfully argued that he should not be held as accountable as other underage teens who have committed vehicular manslaughter while driving under the influence, because Couch grew up so wealthy that he was left with psychological afflictions that made it too difficult to know right from wrong (affluenza).[24] These unjust sentences stand in stark opposition to the overly punitive sentences Black and Brown people are subjected to in our criminal justice system. These biased verdicts are legislative articulations of privilege that sprout from the sinful roots of racism, patriarchy, and classism.

Racial and class disparities are well documented within our criminal justice system,[25] with the death penalty and cocaine sentencing serving as prime examples.[26] When death penalty sentences were applied for rape crimes earlier in the twentieth century, 89 percent of executions were of Black defendants— mostly Black men accused of raping white women.[27] While the rape of a white woman was a capital offense in every slave state, no whites convicted of rape are known to have been executed under these statutes. Additionally, slave owners had the legal right to rape their Black slaves, and the rape of an enslaved Black woman or girl by those who were not her master was considered a property crime.[28] Since then, executions have only been carried out for murder, and 75 percent of convictions resulting in death-penalty sentences have been of white victims—although whites are only slightly more likely to be murder victims.[29] A classic case that crystalized disparities in death penalty sentencing was *McCleskey v. Kemp*. This case proved that Georgia defendants were more than four times as likely to be sentenced to death if the murder victim was white than if the victim was Black.[30]

Until 2010 a five-year mandatory minimum was triggered for the sale of 500 grams of powder cocaine, a drug more typically associated with white users, while the sale of 5 grams of crack, a drug more typically associated with Black and Hispanic users, triggered the same sentence. In 2010 this gross disparity was finally addressed by Congress, but only partially. The Fair Sentencing Act (FSA) reduced the sentencing disparity from 100:1 to 18:1. Consequently, a stark racial disparity persists.[31]

Leveraging versus Abandoning

Having privilege is not a sin, though sin has perverted our systems and structures in ways that engender sinful disparities. Privilege creates and expands anti-gospel inequities that infringe on collective liberation and shalom. It endows a few with educational, socioeconomic, political, vocational, and other advantages while disenfranchising many—simply because of how God intentionally created them.

While we cannot control how we are born, and therefore some of the privileges we are endowed with in a world marred by sin, we can and must—if we are going to have integrity—acknowledge that privilege emerges from ancestral sin and is reified in the systems and institutions we uphold today. Unequivocally proclaiming that privilege is a distortion of God's will frees us from being captive to it. Our Creator never intended for the divine image to be affirmed, respected, and protected in some more than others because of a person's race, ethnicity, gender, class, citizenship status, land of origin, sexuality, mental cognition, able-bodiedness, and physical attractiveness.

When we can confess the sins that breed privilege and renounce the inequities it engenders, then, and only then, can we understand privilege—and the unique access it grants—as a subversive tool that can be leveraged to further the kingdom and love our neighbors. Building from this foundation, privilege becomes a unique opportunity for us to bear witness to who and whose we are. When we leverage privilege instead of exploiting it, we function as the leaven in the loaf, the moral compass and accountability in spaces and places of distinction.

Proverbs 31:8–9, where King Lemuel's mother gives him instruction on how to be a righteous king, gives us a picture of what privilege should be used to do. It reads, "Speak up for those who cannot speak for themselves, for the rights of all who are destitute. Speak up and judge fairly; defend the rights of the poor and needy."

Since privilege is stackable (meaning we can hold many different forms simultaneously) and various forms of privilege have different manifestations, there are two categories of privilege: those we can renounce and those we cannot fully forsake.

How we steward the privileges we can renounce reveals whether we believe we serve a God of scarcity or abundance—one who has created enough for everyone's needs but not enough for all our greed.

Economic privilege, for instance, enables some the luxury of choosing where to live. Christians with economic privilege need to ask challenging questions to ensure we are not exploiting our privilege for selfish gain.

Does where I live . . .

- prohibit me (and my family) from being proximate to the least of these?
  - Does this lack of proximity breed indifference toward their plight?
  - Does this lack of proximity hinder me/us from loving our vulnerable neighbors well?
- disconnect me (and my family) from the pain of my people?
  - Has this disconnect caused me/us to choose individual freedom over collective liberation?
  - Amid this disconnect, can I truly tell if the Spirit reveals that I am still not free?
- reflect the mosaic nature of the kingdom?
  - If not, how does this shape my racial and economic imagination (and my children's)?
  - Does this prohibit me/us from authentically pursuing the kingdom on earth as it is in heaven?
  - If diversity is a revelatory gift from God, what revelation am I missing out on when I choose homogeneity?

- provide room to shelter a neighbor in need?
  - How do passages like Acts 2:42–47; 1 John 3:16–18; and Luke 3:10–11 inform how I steward what I have been entrusted with?
  - How do the stories of the rich young ruler and Zacchaeus inform my understanding of kingdom economics?

There are more questions to ponder, especially if we live within a gentrifying community:

- Do I send my child to the neighborhood school?
  - If I do not send my child to the local school or shop at our local grocery store, what does this communicate to my neighbors?
  - And more importantly, how am I intentionally investing in the flourishing of the local school and neighborhood in which I reside if I choose to send my child, and spend my money, elsewhere?

When we see our access, assets, education, resources, status, social capital, talents, and wealth as solely for our benefit or the enrichment of our family, we sin because we exploit our privilege for selfish gain and therefore refuse to participate in the economy of the kingdom and the inbreaking reign of God. We are called to prayerfully discern how we can relinquish privileges that can be divested as an act of loving obedience to God, in sacrificial fellowship with our neighbors.

There are some privileges we cannot forsake. We are born in a certain place, in a particular body, with certain capacities and genes. I, for instance, cannot completely abandon my maleness—and consequently the privileges it engenders.[32] I can, however, intentionally leverage these privileges for justice when I am in relationships of accountability with my sisters. I can discern with them how I go about leveraging my influence, platform, and voice to advocate for institutional accountability, change, and equity. I can learn from my sisters how I can advocate on their behalf in helpful ways—not as a male savior—when they are not present, I can boycott organizations that desire my voice while excluding theirs, and I can recommend my sisters anytime I get asked for recommendations.

However, when I understand my male privilege as the rotten fruit of my ancestors' sins, I am called to even more. With relational accountability and transparency, I can intentionally invest in women of color, who are dually oppressed and are constantly overlooked for leadership development and mentoring opportunities because of things like the Billy Graham Rule, where men almost exclusively focus on discipling and investing in other men to "avoid any situation that would have even the appearance of compromise or suspicion."[33] I can dedicate a portion of the proceeds garnered from my platform to invest in the flourishing and platform expansion of women of color. I can also be intentional about submitting to the leadership of women of color.

In keeping with repentance for the sin of patriarchy, which I did not create but I do benefit from, I can bear kingdom fruit by discipling other men to dismantle patriarchy, leverage male privilege, and discern how they, too, can produce fruit in keeping with repentance. I can investigate why so few sisters are at tables of power; use my platform to uplift how Scripture calls us to affirm, see, and treat women; and publicly acknowledge the indispensable role women have played in my own discipleship and faith formation. I can also humbly and publicly confess when I get it wrong and commit to doing and being better without making excuses.

Unmasking Privilege

Satan uses privilege as a constant temptation, baiting believers away from the will of God into sin and self-centeredness. What we do with privilege is a spiritual battle, one we are incapable of winning in our own strength. We need the Holy Spirit and the mindset of Christ to overcome the evil one, just as Jesus did in the desert. When we take on the mindset of Christ, empowered by the Spirit, we will rebuke Satan and overcome the temptation to exploit privilege for selfish gain. When we do not, we succumb to sin, exploit privilege, and ignore the anguished cries of our neighbors, turning a blind eye to their suffering to sustain the privileges we have chosen.

Scripture repeatedly acknowledges privilege, which helps provide insight into how privilege insidiously functions today. Learning to unmask privilege is painful work, but the cure for the pain is in the pain. By candidly addressing privilege, we create a unique opportunity for the body of Christ to turn away from sin and reorient ourselves toward God and neighbor. The spiritual disciplines of remembrance, confession, lament, and repentance allow us to discern what producing fruit in keeping with repentance entails. Denying that privilege exists only exacerbates the evil it produces and prohibits us from actively participating as colaborers with Christ in reconciling the world to God.

While we often do not commit the sins that induce privilege, we are responsible for mending the wounds these transgressions continue to cause. We cannot passively benefit from sin and faithfully follow Jesus. Scripture highlights a multitude of faithful women and men who bore a subversive witness. They model how we can leverage what we have been entrusted with to advance the kingdom and love our neighbors.

God knows how challenging it is to be a subversive witness, and that is why Jesus sent us an advocate! As you read this book and learn about how various figures from Scripture stewarded their privilege to further the kingdom and love their neighbor, open yourself up to the restorative power of the Spirit, which moves us to love sacrificially beyond our human limitations.

Reflection Questions

1. How does unchecked privilege foster mythology? Where have you seen it embolden an ahistorical theology and worldviews?
2. How are truth and reconciliation related?
3. What privileges do you possess? Remember that privilege comes in many forms.
4. How can acknowledging and addressing privilege liberate us from its power? If you feel stuck, revisit the introduction to recall how church leadership addressed privilege in Acts 6:1–7.
5. How have you seen Satan use privilege to bait believers away from the will of God into sin and self-centeredness?
6. Why is it tempting to deny that privilege exists?

CHAPTER 2

PHARAOH'S DAUGHTER

Leveraging Privilege to
Resist Systemic Sin

> *We need leaders not in love with money but*
> *in love with justice. Not in love with publicity*
> *but in love with humanity. Leaders who can*
> *subject their particular egos to the pressing*
> *urgencies of the great cause of freedom. . . . A*
> *time like this demands great leaders.*
> —Martin Luther King Jr.,
> "The Birth of a New Age" [1]

Great leadership makes all the difference in the world! Great leaders are humble yet confident, teachable yet wise, compassionate, and strong. Great leaders bring the best out of others and lead out of a deep love for people. Leading by example, they demonstrate that a servant's heart is a hallmark of an effective leader. As Christians, we know that great leaders strive to pray without ceasing, foster a conscious dependence on the Holy Spirit, and pattern their lives after Jesus. Hosea 4:6 explains that God's people perish because of a lack of knowledge, and the masses also suffer when they lack godly leadership.

Narcissistic political leaders fear losing their power, influence, and possessions more than they fear God. Their insecurities lure them into idolatry, fear distorts their vision, and paranoia prohibits them from affirming the *imago Dei* inherent in all their neighbors. Consequently, their dictates exacerbate existing chasms between the privileged and disenfranchised.

Immoral leaders understand that when marginalized people are politically diagnosed as a social albatross, it becomes acceptable—if not patriotic—to vilify them, infringe on their human rights, and become apathetic toward their plight. Thus these leaders strategically enact sinful legislation that systemically targets, oppresses, and scapegoats the most vulnerable. They then begin to sedate the morality of the majority by clandestinely deploying propaganda—which becomes more overt over time—that demonizes the least of these. This tactical approach was deployed against Jewish, mentally and physically impaired, and Afro-German people under the Nazi regime in Germany; Bosniak (Bosnian Muslim) and Croatian civilians leading up to and during the Bosnian genocide; Aboriginal people in Australia during the Vandemonian War; and Indigenous, Black, Asian, and Latino/a/x American communities in the US under various administrations.

While propaganda is always contextual—meaning it is articulated, distributed, and institutionalized in nuanced ways to resonate where it is spewed—the end goal is consistent. Leaders use propaganda to convince the masses that there is a common enemy, an *us versus them*, and that if we can get rid of or keep *them* subjugated, then *we* will flourish, thrive, and enjoy abundant life. The vilified group is almost always depicted as dangerous, a drain on the economy, or uncivilized, and sometimes all three. Leaders who exploit their power in this manner have legacies marked by greed, coercion, and violence. Biblically, the pharaoh of the exodus period epitomized this type of leadership, and Exodus 1:6–22; 2:1–10 illuminates the social implications of his political reign.

In this passage the Hebrews are ethnically profiled, dehumanized, and enslaved simply because of Pharaoh's fear. His anxiety seduces him into passing oppressive legislation that scapegoats and persecutes Hebrews. As Pharaoh's fear of the growing Hebrew population intensifies, he becomes despotic and establishes a totalitarian regime. Ultimately, he becomes so tyrannical that he commands the Hebrew midwives to murder all newborn Hebrew boys. Describing the civil disobedience of Shiphrah and Puah, Old Testament scholar Terence Fretheim writes, Pharaoh "can get the entire Egyptian community to bend to his will but fails to get two daughters of Israel to so respond."[2] When the midwives refuse his direct decree, "When you are helping the Hebrew women during childbirth on the delivery stool, if you see that the baby is a boy, kill him; but if it is a girl, let her live" (Ex. 1:16), he does not respond by merely killing or imprisoning them. He responds by legally requiring the entire nation to participate in an ethnic infanticide. Pharaoh's fear drives him to sin, and his individual sin becomes institutionalized and inscribed into law. When this transpires, the entire Egyptian Empire is led astray, and his constituents become complicit. When government officials lack the maturity to address their sin and do not have the integrity to surround themselves with others who will, their individual sin usually leads those they govern into corporate sin.

Pharaohs Need Consent

Egypt was a theocratic monarchy, a form of government in which a deity is recognized as the supreme civil ruler, and the deity's laws are interpreted by the ecclesiastical authorities. The US, on the other hand, is a constitutional federal republic, a form of government in which a representative is elected by the people to govern over them according to the rules established in the law of the land. Yet in both forms of government, the people's consent and compliance are what ultimately legitimates the leader's power.

While Pharaoh must be held accountable for his immorality and oppression, pointing the finger at him alone is insufficient. Exclusively focusing on Pharaoh absolves the rest of Egypt. It divests citizens of their political autonomy and allows the masses to claim, "We just followed the chain of command." This corporate cop-out is played out![3]

We need a deeper analysis, one that requires us to acknowledge that ultimately pharaohs have only the power that we, as consenting constituents, give them. Therefore, rather than focus on the individual—and again, this is not to pardon unethical leaders in any way—let us reckon with the collective response of Egypt.

Amid the rampant oppression, dehumanization, and killing that occur in the first chapter of Exodus, Scripture does not note a single Egyptian who stands up to, speaks out against, or refuses to obey Pharaoh's sinful legislation. Why is that? Given the depth of barbarism, exploitation, and murder, there must have been at least a few Egyptians who objected to Pharaoh's sinful reign on ethical and moral grounds. But, if this were the case, why did they choose to acquiesce?

Within a theocracy like the Egyptian Empire, the answer is likely religious manipulation. People are told, and often believe, that leaders are divinely appointed—even when their leadership does not align with the values or principles of their faith. When the masses believe a leader is chosen by God, many in turn believe that the leader can do no wrong. Moreover, many may also believe that they would become wrong themselves if they opposed the will or policies of a God-appointed leader. Therefore people commonly comply even when they internally question a leader's choices. Within a totalitarian regime, people commonly feel coerced into compliance. They obey out of sheer fear of retribution. When this happens, out of self-preservation, people consciously participate in immorality because they are summoned to. But regardless of why people comply, it is their choice to make.

What keeps good people silent and complicit when they know their neighbor is being dehumanized, oppressed, exploited, and/or massacred? We seldomly ask this pointed question within our sermons, Bible studies, and quiet times with God. However, this is one of the most urgent questions of our time, and the gospel demands an answer! Unfortunately, passages like this one in Exodus that provoke this vital question are usually interpreted in ways that do not compel us to reckon with how our silence sanctions oppression.

Lamentably, instead of being the salt and light of the

world—demonstrating that we are Christ's disciples by expressing countercultural love for one another—we have all too often subscribed to the self-serving ethic of the Egyptians in this passage. While there is indeed no condemnation for those who are in Christ Jesus (Rom. 8:1), Scripture gives repeated commissions to participate actively and sacrificially in God's reconciling love. Christ gave us a new commandment—to love one another as he has loved us. First John 3:16 explains, "This is how we know what love is: Jesus Christ laid down his life for us. And we ought to lay down our lives for our brothers and sisters." And the apostle Paul, in Galatians 5:6, declares that "the only thing that counts is faith expressing itself through love." Furthermore, 2 Corinthians 5:20 tells us that "we are therefore Christ's ambassadors, as though God were making his appeal through us."

Consequently, when we choose silence, apathy, and inaction in the face of oppression because *we* are not directly harmed by it or because *we* reap benefits from it, we are being disobedient to Scripture. The complicit have blood on their hands along with the unethical political leaders and bigoted individuals who intentionally stoke the flames of oppression, xenophobia, and racism.

When Christians blindly follow elected leaders who they know are defacing the *imago Dei* in their neighbors, they declare that they have given their allegiance to a flag instead of to God's kingdom. When the blood of our neighbor cries out from the ground, privileged parts of the body—who are unaffected by the death and oppression their neighbors endure—are tempted to believe that choosing to avoid conflict, keeping "political matters" outside church, and "minding my own business" are not sinful, self-centered responses. When Christians become conformed to the pattern of this world, we find it easy to denounce other individuals who zealously participate in oppression but extremely difficult to see our own complicity within unjust systems, structures, and regimes. While there has always been a faithful remnant within the body of Christ in oppressive contexts, the broader church has overwhelmingly shied away from Scripture's call to sacrificially love our neighbor as ourselves—particularly across lines of difference.

Therefore, in the US, the question must be asked frankly, where was the church's outcry and resistance to unethical leaders amid Indigenous genocide, boarding schools, and treaty breaches; slavery, lynching, and Jim Crow; yellow peril, Chinese exclusion, and Japanese incarceration camps; the Bracero program, Operation Wetback, and the farmworkers movement? Beyond the parts of the body directly impacted by these racial and ethnic atrocities, where was the witness of the church? How did Christians bear witness to the love of God when it was most needed? Furthermore, what have we learned from these missteps? Is our collective witness in the face of oppression any different today than it was for our ancestors? As COVID-19 xenophobia rises, anti-Asian hate crimes increase; families are separated at our southern border; Black people continue to be criminalized and overincarcerated; and native women are being abducted, assaulted, and murdered, it seems like we continue to miss the point of passages like Exodus 1:6–22.

Lamentably, in oppressive contexts, many people have come to expect Christians to choose privilege, self-centeredness, and allegiance to worldly empires over sacrificial love and justice. To change this legacy, we must confess, lament, and recommit ourselves to producing fruit in keeping with repentance. The second chapter of Exodus illustrates what this entails.

Wade in the Water

Chapter 2 opens with Moses' birth, which leaves his mom, Jochebed, in an insufferable situation. She can either obey the law—which requires her son to be killed because of his ethnicity—or break it. Jochebed's love compels her to become a "criminal." She chooses to save Moses and then hides him for three months until he is too large to conceal. Forced to confront her human limitations in an oppressive context, Jochebed, in an act of utter desperation, creates a makeshift papyrus basket and coats it with tar and pitch.

She places Moses inside the basket, puts the basket in the Nile River, and fully entrusts her beloved son to God. Old Testament scholar James Bruckner writes that Jochebed's coating of Moses' "'basket' (*tebah*) or 'ark' with 'pitch' fulfills the instructions given to Noah for the 'ark' (*tebah*; Gen. 6:14; 7:7). In both cases the word means 'a chest' or 'container in which something precious is stored.' The baby's basket was an ark of salvation for the boy. As with Noah, the salvation of humanity depended on this little ark."[4] Bruckner then explains, "The 'tar' (*khemar*) or 'plaster' that sealed the basket ark also carries literary weight, as the 'mortar' (1:14) with which the laborers toiled is the same word. The same substance Pharaoh used as means of oppression, a mother's hands spread as an agent of salvation."[5]

Placing Moses in the Nile was extremely risky, but unlike Pharaoh, Jochebed was not controlled by fear. Jochebed's decision in the face of fear demonstrates her belief in God's sovereignty. The basket could have sprung a leak or tipped over. Moses could have drowned, been eaten by a wild creature, or been found by someone who wished to do him harm. Instead, the Spirit of God protected and guided the basket to what seemed to be the worst place it could have docked: the banks of Pharaoh's palace, where the decree to kill Moses originated.

Imagine the anxiety Miriam (Moses' sister) felt—standing at a distance, trying to safeguard her brother—as Pharaoh's daughter discovered his basket. Miriam probably dropped to her knees in prayer, crying out to God, asking for divine intervention. Miriam knew Pharaoh's daughter had been raised in a house of bigotry. Pharaoh's daughter had been discipled by her father to see Hebrews as subhuman and disposable; their only value lay in their free labor. She had been trained to see Hebrews as her enemies and was warned that if they were not contained, ruthlessly overseen, and hegemonically governed, all the privileges and comforts she had become accustomed to would end.

Pharaoh's daughter instructed her female slave to retrieve the basket and bring it to her. She opened it, saw Moses crying, and had compassion for him. Then she said, "This is one of the Hebrew babies." This is one of the most riveting scenes in Scripture. As Moses' life hung in the balance, Pharaoh's daughter found herself confounded by the power of proximity and its ability to transform her vision and the ways in which she had conformed to the pattern of this world. Pharaoh's daughter was discipled to be xenophobic. She was raised in a context that celebrated and rewarded ethnic bias, enmity, and oppression. She was groomed by a father with deeply engrained prejudices, who surely intended to pass these beliefs down to his children and certainly spewed vitriol and propaganda amid family gatherings. She was primed to carry on the family tradition of hatred.

God's Gonna Trouble the Water

Pharaoh's daughter knew what she was supposed to do if she encountered a Hebrew boy. His very existence was evidence of lawlessness and an insubordinate Hebrew parent. Yet, as she stood in the water with all this knowledge, she was unaware of the presence of the Spirit of God hovering over the water, bringing chaos into order by transforming her vison and bringing forth a new ethic of belonging, a foretaste of the *coming* kingdom. Hence, when Pharaoh's daughter opened the basket and looked into Moses' eyes, she did not see what she expected to see: a threat, an enemy, someone whose life did not matter. Her feelings were not what she may have anticipated: repulsion, disdain, and the hatred her father coerced her to feel. Instead, she felt compassion. Whether she realized it or not, God revealed to her that Moses had inherent value as another human being. Though she may not have had the words for it, we know this is because Moses was also made in the image of God. Subsequently, instead of Pharaoh's daughter operating out of the us-versus-them ethos of empire, the Spirit started to renew her mind, which enabled her to begin to understand that her humanity was ultimately tied to Moses'.

God's work, however, was not confined to the water. Knowing that the renewal of Pharaoh's daughter's mind was just beginning, the Spirit subversively worked through Miriam, who recognized the opportunity to influence what happened to Moses. She swiftly interjected herself into the plot as Pharaoh's daughter was trying to make sense of the transformation she was experiencing. Miriam cleverly offered to find a Hebrew woman to nurse Moses—because in that context it would have been unfathomable for an Egyptian woman to nurse him. Pharaoh's daughter agreed, and we see God orchestrate this circumstance in a way that only God could: by enabling the very empire that severed Moses' mother from her beloved son to pay her to raise him. Speaking of the work of the Spirit through Jochebed, Miriam, and Pharaoh's daughter, Fretheim writes, "In the end, three daughters bring the son through death to life."[6]

The Spirit's work in Pharaoh's daughter did not end that day. She not only broke the law to spare Moses' life, but she disobeyed her father's orders—putting his reputation and credibility on the line and causing a scandalous social disruption by seeing herself as bound to an "inferior" Hebrew.

Furthermore, after initially outsourcing his care, she brought Moses into her father's house and raised him as her own son. Understand the audacity this took and everything she risked in making this countercultural decision. She could have been disowned by her father, cut off from his wealth, as well as the privilege it afforded, and imprisoned, if not killed. If word got out that Pharaoh's own daughter had not obeyed his orders and the law, he would have become a laughingstock and lost some of his power and influence.

Nevertheless, despite what this decision could have cost her and the fear she likely had as she made it, she followed the Spirit's conviction to do what was right and to prove herself faithful. Pharaoh's daughter subversively acted, defying her earthly father in obedience to the Holy Spirit. However, she did not realize the helpless baby she saved wasn't just any Hebrew boy, but the one God chose to liberate Israel from slavery and destroy her father's oppressive empire.[7]

This story is good news. It demonstrates that the gospel has the power to break generational cycles of bigotry. It bears witness to the fact that the Spirit can transform those most ensconced in bias and immersed in injustice. And it shows that freedom and liberation are possibilities for everyone, even those who descend from families who have devoted themselves to sinful ideologies of supremacy and have enacted systemic oppression and social injustice. It affirms that God is truly with us amid our suffering and that oppression, death, and sin truly do not have the last word. When God seems to be silent, our sovereign Savior is still at work, moving to make a way out of no way. And while trying times do not always have a happy ending like this one, could that say more about us as the people of God—and our apathy regarding our neighbors suffering—than it does about God's sovereignty?

The theological implications of this passage are immense. Pharaoh's daughter transgressed ethnic and class boundaries of belonging. She intimately identified with "the other" in treasonous ways. This prophetic act of faithfulness could have cost her everything. Nevertheless, she remained faithful to what she knew was right, even in the face of all that was at risk. Within this perilous interaction, lines of belonging, purity, and family are all fundamentally reconstructed. A kingdom vision of belonging begins to emerge, one that does not subscribe to the imperial logic of "us" and "them," haves and have-nots, or clean and unclean. This kingdom ethic of belonging has been misinterpreted by many scholars, theologians, and preachers as something God started in the New Testament, but it actually is something that God has been willing and bringing into fruition since the garden. These interpreters of Scripture have merely lacked eyes to see it.

Bruckner writes, "The saving of Moses from the edict of Pharaoh is paradigmatic. It foreshadows God saving Israel from the violence of Pharaoh at the crossing of the Red Sea. Matthew 2 echoes this salvation story—a son who would be born, laid in a rough bassinet by a lowly mother, and survives the senseless murder of children by a violent king."[8] Moses and Jesus are emancipators bound by the Spirit of God, the oppressive empires they were born into, and the subversive witness of their mothers. Jochebed and Mary engaged in civil disobedience that is indispensable to our faith. Their resistance paved the way for their sons to grow up and enact deliverance for the children of God. The Spirit led Jochebed, Mary, Moses, and Jesus to prophetically resist evil, and their obedience to the Spirit made salvation, reconciliation, and liberation possible for us.

The Cost of Discipleship

This passage lays bare a central question that is at the heart of Scripture, one the Bible consistently poses yet we frequently try to avoid: Is the gospel still good news when it costs you something? Moreover, when bearing witness to the gospel could cost you everything, as it could have for Pharaoh's daughter, do we still consider this news good? When we study a text like this Exodus passage and do not walk away with application questions like these, we are missing the point of Scripture and stifling the Spirit at work within our sacred text. When we fail to grapple with the cost of discipleship and the ethical implications a text like this should have on our spiritual formation, we embolden our members to mistake silence, inaction, and "apolitical" responses in the face of oppression as faithfulness to God. When we truly allow God's Word to be a lamp unto our feet and a light unto our path, we will truly have to reckon with the deadly costs of silence, protecting privilege, and giving our allegiance to worldly empires.

Pharaoh's daughter becomes a model for us regarding how one responsibly stewards privilege for the furtherance of the kingdom and the good of neighbor. What starts as compassion grows into conviction and matures into a rigorous commitment to justice. We see the fruit of this maturation in the life of Moses and the selfless, God-honoring decisions he grows up to make. Moses did not make these faithful, sacrificial decisions on his own; he was discipled by both of his mothers in an understanding of what faithfulness entails.

Finally, lest we forget, Pharaoh's daughter—as much as she should be revered—had the opportunity to be transformed only because of Jochebed's faithfulness and the faithfulness of the Hebrew midwives before her. These women's nonviolent civil disobedience created a divine opportunity for Pharaoh's daughter to be confronted with her sinful complicity.

Terence Fretheim describes the "divine irony" flowing though this passage, highlighting how God used what Pharaoh saw as weak, what the empire saw as lowly and despised, to shame the strong (cf. Jer. 9:23; 1 Cor. 1:26–29). Fretheim writes, "Rather than using power as it is usually exercised in the world,

God works through persons who have no obvious power; indeed, they are unlikely candidates for the exercise of power. . . . But they prove highly effective against the ruthless forms of systemic power."[9] James Bruckner affirms this interpretation, writing, "The midwives' courage and fear of the Lord contrast with the powerful, yet paranoid, pharaoh. . . . Here we see the beginning of the key role women played in God's deliverance of Israel. . . . The 'power' of the Hebrew midwives, whose names were Shiphrah and Puah, was at once real and tenuous— completely opposite to the power of Pharaoh's violence."[10]

Pharaoh could not fathom a resistance movement led by women. His command, "If you see that the baby is a boy, kill him; but if it is a girl, let her live," exemplifies this. Bruckner describes the irony of this decree: "Pharaoh thought men were the threat. In fact, it was women who continued to outfox him."[11] Terence Fretheim writes, "The daughters are allowed to live, and it is they who now proceed to thwart Pharaoh's plans." Finally, Bruckner concludes, "The women of the text play all the decisive roles. Jochebed, Miriam, the daughter of pharaoh. . . . By the end of the story, the pharaoh (who never shows up in this narrative) is thwarted by the women, even as he was by the midwives in Exodus 1."[12] Thank God for the faithfulness of our foremothers and the remnant who refuses to cower before imperial power!

We should be familiar with how civil disobedience can create unique opportunities for divine transformation. We have seen this happen time and time again through the faithful witness of our great-grandparents, abuelas y abuelos, and ummas and appas, all of whom help constitute the great cloud of witnesses. We follow in the footsteps of prophetic leaders like Ella

Baker, Martin Luther King Jr., Ida B. Wells, Cesar Chavez, Óscar Romero, Hélder Câmara, Sharon Maeda, Fred Korematsu, Toyohiko Kagawa, Gordon Hirabayashi, Dorothy Day, Thomas Merton, and André and Magda Trocmé.

While many within the body have become accustomed to seeing nonviolent civil disobedience and the social disruptions these protests cause as sinful, this text—and history—demonstrate that this nature of resistance amid oppression—refusing to obey unjust laws and tyrannical leaders—is faithful to the gospel. Furthermore, God has uniquely used these faithful responses amid evil and oppression to confront those who have been complicit with, and have even driven, oppression, helping them to recognize their sin. This divine revelation has led to confession, lament, and an earnest effort to make amends through bearing fruit in keeping with repentance. The four Hebrew women in the passage and Pharaoh's daughter demonstrate this and give us keen insight into how this plays out.

Reflection Questions

1. How does this passage (Ex. 1:6–22; 2:1–10) help you define and understand privilege?
2. Have you seen political leaders use propaganda to scapegoat, villainize, and/or dehumanize vulnerable people? If so, when?
3. What do you believe keeps good people silent and complicit when they know their neighbor is being dehumanized, oppressed, exploited, and/or massacred?

4. Systemic sin can be challenging for some members of the body to see. Where do you see systemic sin in Exodus 1:6–22; 2:1–10?

5. Have you seen God trouble the waters of belonging, bringing people together across lines of difference in unexpected ways? If so, where and when?

6. Assuming things about people and writing them off can be easy. How does Pharaoh's daughter challenge us to resist these temptations?

CHAPTER 3

ESTHER

Leveraging Privilege to
Stand in Solidarity

The book of Esther begins with King Xerxes throwing an epic party for the nobles and officials of his 127 provinces. This was not just an extravaganza; Xerxes threw a 180-day festival! The celebration was purely to flaunt his power, majesty, and wealth. When the 180-day bash concluded, Xerxes decided to throw a weeklong after-party, with an open bar, for all the men of Susa, Persia's capital city. Men drank without inhibitions and indulged with prostitutes, while their wives attended another party Queen Vashti was throwing in a different section of the palace.

As the after-party concluded, Xerxes—who was completely wasted—thought of a final gesture to display his "preeminence." He ordered his servants to go disrupt the queen's party and bring her before him and his raunchy crowd of inebriated men "wearing her royal crown, in order to display her beauty" (Est. 1:11)—which is to say, Xerxes ordered Vashti to expose and display her body for his ego and his crowd's sexual gratification. Xerxes, therein, dehumanized his wife by ordering her to parade around as merely another one of his possessions. He epitomized toxic masculinity and rape culture by beckoning Vashti into this vile context of degradation where she could be molested, sexually assaulted, and possibly raped. The misogyny undergirding Xerxes's party and his demand of Vashti illuminate that women and marriage vows were not valued within the Persian Empire. Consequently, strong, intelligent, and courageous women like Queen Vashti were reduced to commodities because of society's belief that a woman's value rested in her beauty and ability to sexually satisfy men.

Yet when the king's attendants delivered his command, Queen Vashti refused to come. Knowing the king and the debauchery occurring at his party, Vashti suspected the sexual abuse and violence she would be subjected to. She knew acquiescing to Xerxes's coercive demand would traumatize her for life. In *Becoming Brave*, Brenda Salter McNeil writes, "[Vashti] certainly would have known that she would have to diminish herself and lose her dignity in order to obey the king's orders. She knew what it would mean to parade in front of this group of men. She was being disrespected by the king and would likely be forced into any manner of sexual activity against her will."[1] I imagine it took every ounce of courage Vashti could muster to deny Xerxes, because she knew his temper, ego, and power—intimately. But I thank God that she did! Vashti's resistance to patriarchy serves as a glimmer of hope within a bleak history replete with sexual assault and a Bible littered with accounts of sexual violence. McNeil concludes, "In a time when women had absolutely no agency over their own lives, Vashti took a stand. Harriet Beecher Stowe calls Vashti's disobedience the 'first stand for women's rights.'"[2]

Xerxes became irate when he learned Vashti was not coming. His fragile male ego was crushed, and he felt emasculated in front of his guests. After trying to save face in front of them, Xerxes gathered his good-old-boy network to decide how Vashti must pay for publicly disobeying him. His council—afraid Vashti's protest would empower other women to realize their agency over their bodies—decided that not only must Vashti be dethroned and banished, but her punishment must also serve as a public service announcement to women throughout the region. They banned Vashti from ever entering the king's presence, believing this would remind women throughout the territory of their subservient place and responsibility always, under any circumstance, to submit to and "respect their husbands, from the least to the greatest" (Est. 1:20).

Scholar Bianca Mabute-Louie explains, "The Persian Empire does not value a woman's agency over her own body, nor do they believe women have a right to consent. When a woman says no, she must be punished. In current contexts, this would be interpreted as rape culture: a set of social attitudes and practices that disregard consent in order to normalize and trivialize sexual assault and abuse."[3] This ability to physically and judicially punish, control, and exploit female bodies is patriarchy. Scripture says the king "sent dispatches to all parts of the kingdom, to each province in its own script and to each people in their own language, proclaiming that every man should be ruler over his own household, using his native tongue" (Est. 1:22).

Among other things, the book of Esther summons the church to reckon with patriarchy and its past and present implications.

Same Story, Different Day

The predatory behavior of men like the ones at Xerxes's party has been minimized and explained away for far too long! Euphemisms like "locker room talk" and mantras like "Boys will be boys" embolden sexual assault and domesticate the horrific violation this sin causes. From #MeToo to #ChurchToo, we have begun to see the depth of trauma that survivors are forced to endure, but when will we go upstream to fix the problem? Sexual violence is a discipleship issue, and our unwillingness to address it as such allows too many Christian men and boys to persist in the toxic beliefs that Persian leadership upheld: men are entitled to women's bodies, can take whatever we desire from our spouse or significant other whenever and however we want, and a woman's value lies in her beauty and ability to sexually gratify.

This problem exists inside and outside the church, extending from the Oval Office to college campuses to church youth groups. Victim blaming, blurring the lines of consent, and "blaming it on the alcohol" are ways society shields males from having to confront the trauma our abuse and violence cause. Former President Jimmy Carter declared, "The abuse of women and girls is the most pervasive and unaddressed human rights violation on earth."[4]

It is also imperative to notice how men are spiritually protected in church from having to face our sinful legacy of sexual violence. Pastoral misconduct scandals serve as a primary example of this. Despite how frequent and enduring this nature of abuse is and has been, too many ministers have merely received a slap on the wrist before moving on to continue their work in a new context.

The shield safeguarding men from confronting our sinful legacy of sexual violence flows from the distortion of Scripture. It is a sinister privilege rooted in a history of dominance and exclusion. Men have dominated the field of biblical interpretation, and males have largely ignored, obscured, or mitigated the depth of depravity regarding sexual assault. Rather than candidly confessing our sins, reckoning with our horrid history and the ways Scripture elucidates sexual violence—for example, refusing to explicitly name King David's coerced sexual encounter with Bathsheba as a sexual assault—we have commonly interpreted Scripture in self-serving ways that embolden abuse.

Consequently, too many congregations remain silent about intimate partner violence, molestation, and rape within marriage, despite how prevalent these horrid realities are. The statistics illustrate that these realities are present within our congregations. Our silence on these critical matters has made the church a place where those who enact sexual violence are too comfortable and those who survive it are forced to suffer in isolation.[5]

Jimmy Carter spoke about this, proclaiming, "The truth is that male religious leaders have had—and still have—an option to interpret holy teachings either to exalt or subjugate women. They have, for their own selfish ends, overwhelmingly chosen the latter. Their continuing choice provides the foundation or justification for much of the pervasive persecution and abuse of women throughout the world."[6]

Carter's words ring true anywhere Christians are taught or allowed to read the book of Esther without having to reckon with Queen Vashti's abuse and trauma. Moreover, whenever congregations ignore Queen Vashti's oppression to get to the hope of Esther, we contribute to a culture of sexual violence.

From the Ashes

The book of Esther highlights how important it is to have ethical people in your inner circle. As Xerxes's fury over Vashti's noncompliance subsided, his attendant advised him to abuse his power yet again. He told Xerxes to appoint commissioners in all 127 provinces to traffic beautiful young virgins, forcing them to participate in a toxic competition that did not honor their bodies and personhood. These teenage girls were abducted, taken to the palace, and forced to entertain and sexually satisfy the king. Ultimately, the girl Xerxes was most pleased with would be crowned the new queen. The attendant's advice pleased Xerxes, and he proclaimed an edict initiating it.

At this point in the account we are introduced to Mordecai and his orphaned teenage cousin, Hadassah, who was one of the girls taken to Xerxes. Hadassah and Mordecai were part of a Jewish community living in Susa that never returned to Jerusalem after the Babylonian exile. When Hadassah was taken, Mordecai—who took Hadassah in and raised her when her parents died—told her to conceal her Jewish identity within the palace to prevent persecution. Heeding his instructions, Hadassah, according to author Kathy Khang, transitioned from "a Jewish woman living cross-culturally," who was "known by different names in different circles"[7] to permanently become

Esther to pass as Persian. In Hebrew the root of *Esther* is *hester*, which means "hidden."[8] Empires coerce people—especially vulnerable individuals—to hide, suppress, and deny parts of who they truly are. Empires flourish when marginalized people are stripped of their culture, language, and traditions.

The trafficked teenage girls were pampered upon arrival at the palace. They were given beauty treatments—aromatherapy, perfumes, and cosmetics for an entire year—in preparation for their one night of horror with the king. This is an age-old imperial ploy. Empires do not just brutalize; they also gratify to pacify. As Walter Brueggemann explains in his seminal text *The Prophetic Imagination,* "Imperial economics is designed to keep people satiated so they do not notice. Its politics is intended to block out the cries of the denied ones. Its religion is to be an opiate so that no one discerns misery alive in the heart of God."[9] The lavish pampering and luxurious living during the year prior to being sexually assaulted by the king was intended to mute the cries of teenage virgins who lacked the power to exercise autonomy over their bodies. The empire nullified consent, and Scripture explains that a girl "would not return to the king unless he was pleased with her and summoned her by name" (Est. 2:14).

During Esther's time of "preparation," Mordecai paced the palace grounds daily, trying to ensure her safety. His anxiety likely grew out of his fear—regarding Esther's ability to successfully keep her Jewish identity concealed and the sexual violation he knew she would endure. Nevertheless, as was the case with Jochebed, imperial oppression rendered Mordecai powerless to protect his beloved, and he, too, would have to fully entrust his beloved to God.

Esther was strikingly beautiful, and her beauty helped her gain favor in the palace. However, she was also a brilliant and resilient girl, and many theologians have failed to adequately accredit her these virtues. To pass as Persian in the palace, Esther's language and cultural competency must have been impeccable. Furthermore, to navigate these challenges as a teenager who endured ethnic persecution, trauma, and the loss of her parents is a testament to her character and resilience. These qualities and Vashti's civil disobedience made it possible for Esther to become queen.

Shortly after Esther became queen, Mordecai was sitting at the king's gate and overheard two of Xerxes's officials conspiring to assassinate the king. Mordecai told Esther, who informed Xerxes, and after the plot was confirmed, Mordecai was credited with saving the king's life. Chapter 2 ends with Mordecai's heroism being documented in the royal book of the annals.

The king appointed a new right-hand man as chapter 3 begins, and surprisingly, it was not Mordecai. Instead, we are introduced to Haman the Agagite. Scholar Timothy Cain explains, "Any Jew would have immediately seen the irony. Not only does Mordecai get passed up, but the king promotes Haman the Agagite. This is significant because Agagites are descendants of Amalekites, who are ancient tribal enemies of Jews."[10] The king did not just promote Haman, but he enacted a law requiring anyone in Haman's presence to kneel before him in honor. Mordecai, a devout Jew—like his ancestors Hananiah, Mishael, and Azariah, or as most know them, Shadrach, Meshach, and Abednego—refused to kneel before and give honor to anyone other than God. Haman was infuriated by

Mordecai's refusal to bow to him. Scripture reads, "Having learned who Mordecai's people were, he scorned the idea of killing only Mordecai. Instead Haman looked for a way to destroy all Mordecai's people, the Jews, throughout the whole kingdom of Xerxes" (Est. 3:6).

Haman, embarrassed and incensed, went to Xerxes and spewed propaganda in hopes of inaugurating a genocide. Haman, a foreigner himself, described Jews as criminals and separatists who were too culturally different to ever fit in— perpetual foreigners. He told the king that the very presence of Jews could undermine the Persian Empire and advised Xerxes to exterminate them. Haman's anti-Semitism ran so deep, it provoked him to volunteer to finance this racial cleansing.

> "There is a certain people dispersed among the peoples in all the provinces of your kingdom who keep themselves separate. Their customs are different from those of all other people, and they do not obey the king's laws; it is not in the king's best interest to tolerate them. If it pleases the king, let a decree be issued to destroy them, and I will give ten thousand talents of silver to the king's administrators for the royal treasury."
>
> So the king took his signet ring from his finger and gave it to Haman son of Hammedatha, the Agagite, the enemy of the Jews. "Keep the money," the king said to Haman, "and do with the people as you please." (Est. 3:8–11)

Unconcerned about a "disposable" minority group and unaware that his wife was a part of that group, the king told Haman to keep his money and granted his wish. The two then celebrated this murderous decree by getting drunk. How do people craft legislation to annihilate others and sleep at night?

As the decree was spread throughout the land, Esther found herself cloistered in the luxuries of the palace, her privilege blinding her to the imminent demise of her people. After nearly eight years as queen, immersed in the extravagance of the palace, Esther had become disconnected from reality and the pain of her people. As Esther was satiated, lavishing in luxury, her people were fasting, weeping, and wailing in despair.

Lamentation Leads to Repentance

When Mordecai heard about the Jewish genocide, he ripped his clothes, put on sackcloth and ashes, and went out into the city inconsolably wailing. Walter Brueggemann, highlighting the role public lament plays in Christianity, writes that in our public lament, "it is made clear that things are not as they should be, not as they were promised, and not as they must be. Bringing hurt to public expression is an important first step in the dismantling criticism that permits a new reality, theological and social, to emerge."[11] Understanding this concept, empires are hell-bent on suppressing public lament, regardless of the form it takes: marches, civil disobedience, nonviolent protests, sit-ins, or prayer vigils. Scripture attests this truth, saying, "But he [Mordecai] went only as far as the king's gate, because no one clothed in sackcloth was allowed to enter it" (Est. 4:2). Brueggemann explains that this rule was made because "kings would do everything but grieve, for that is the ultimate criticism and the decisive announcement of dismantling. . . . Weeping is something kings rarely do without losing their thrones."[12]

Consequently, kings outlaw public lament, and prohibit anyone seeking to inspire or encourage it from entering their midst.

Churches have also prohibited lament. We saw this happen as the #ChurchToo movement grew. Many survivors and allies mobilized to create ecclesial space to address sexual violence, toxic masculinity, and patriarchy. All too often these voices were silenced as they tried to create systems of accountability and spaces for healing and restoration. This was a missed opportunity for confessing, lamenting, and repenting. Since we did not do these things, many survivors continue to suffer in unnecessary isolation and shame. When Esther initially heard about Mordecai's lamentation outside the king's gate, she sent him clothes to put on in exchange for his sackcloth, but Mordecai refused them. Though she was probably well intentioned—hoping to draw attention from her uncle to prevent his persecution for protesting—by sending clothes to alter, if not silence, Mordecai's lamentation, Esther enacted what the prophet Jeremiah criticized in Jeremiah 6:14: "They dress the wound of my people as though it were not serious. 'Peace, peace,' they say, when there is no peace."

Only after seeing Mordecai reject her offering and persist in his lament did Esther seek to find out why he was protesting and what provoked his anguish. This, unfortunately, is all too often the response of privileged believers today too. The initial response to violated people is to ask those who are viscerally crying out to God to alter or repackage their public lament in a more palatable manner. Then, and only then, do privileged Christians usually start inquiring about the lament and seeking to understand what provoked it. This is an unfaithful response to the gospel of Jesus Christ and the suffering of our neighbors.

Too many congregations have taken this posture in response to the Black Lives Matter movement. Instead of taking on the mindset of Christ, assuming a Philippians 2 posture[13] of humbly listening and learning, then sacrificially seeking the interest of others first, these churches have commonly turned a deaf ear to the lamentations of their wounded neighbors.

As protests affirming the inherent dignity of Black lives evolved into a global movement, too many congregations used their influence to denounce and delegitimate peaceful protest. These churches missed precious opportunities to be ambassadors of reconciliation by demonstrating the love of God in response to human harm. As heartbroken people wept and wailed in the streets, petitioning the Lord to intervene with righteousness and justice, many of us feared for our lives and the future of our children. We prayed Psalm 13:1, asking, "How long, LORD? Will you forget me forever? How long will you hide your face from me?" Instead of working to build a more just and equitable society, too many churches vilified nonviolent protest and focused their energy and resources on winning a culture war. I have shed many a tear over how many people have walked away from the church and the faith because of this ecclesial response.

Transformational Power in Lament

Our faith becomes anemic when lament becomes optional. Lamentation prevents us from becoming numb and apathetic to the pain of our world. Scripture describes lamentation as a liturgical act that reorients and transforms us.

Lament is a space where we viscerally worship and learn to be honest, vulnerable, and humble before God. When we lament, we confess our humanity and depravity. Lamentation is an anguished acknowledgment that things are not as they should be, a tormented wail beckoning the Lord to intervene with righteousness and justice. When we lament, we confess our need for a Savior, conceding that we are too weak to combat the powers, principalities, and spiritual wickedness on our own. Our lamentations declare that only God has the power to truly end oppression, mend brokenness, and restore what sin has perverted.

As never before in history, we are bombarded by an unprecedented, unceasing stream of media that exposes us to the world's pain and brokenness. Before we have the chance to authentically grieve one tragedy, another occurs. So, in a rush to keep up with our newsfeeds and the newest hashtag, casualty captured on video, sexual assault scandal, or governmental official espousing racial slurs, we move on before processing the trauma we have just witnessed.

Lamentation, however, forces us to slow down. Amid unrelenting trauma and tragedy, lament requires us to stay engaged after the cameras and publicity move on. It summons us to immerse ourselves in the pain and despair of the world, of our nation, of our communities.

We lament because, paradoxically, the cure for the pain is in the pain. Lamentation begets revelation. It opens our eyes to death, oppression, and systemic sin we have failed to notice. It attunes our ears to the torture, anguish, and weeping that has become white noise in our fractured world. Lamentation is a spiritual practice that softens hardened hearts, a revolutionary act that ushers us into uncensored communion with God. As a Christian, to live without lament is to live an unexamined life.

Without history and proximity, lamentation seems unwarranted. No one laments what they do not know, and most people gloss over statistics that they cannot associate faces with—regardless of how heartbreaking the stats are. Lamentation compels us to expose what the empire seeks to conceal and deny. It emboldens us to see suffering anew, speak truth to power, and draw near to our neighbors on the margins. When the church takes history seriously, lament will become requisite. We will in turn learn to dignify, remember, and learn from the exterminated, demarcated, and violated bodies of our nation's past and present.

When faithfully engaged and authentically enacted, lamentation keeps us accountable to our baptismal vows. It reminds us of our need for God, one another, and the Spirit's guidance. Lamentation is a spiritual practice that shapes our discipleship and missiology; it illuminates blind spots in our lives and ministry, helping us to make our witness more Christlike and our evangelism more contextual, holistic, and responsible.

Remembrance should lead to confession, and confession is meant to engender lamentation. However, Soong-Chan Rah, in *Prophetic Lament*, finds that privilege hinders lament, as we see in Esther's response to the killing of her people. Rah writes, "The American church avoids lament. The power of lament is minimized and the underlying narrative of suffering that requires lament is lost."[14] Rah then explains that we forsake lament because "true reconciliation, justice and shalom require a remembering of suffering, an unearthing of a shameful history."[15] Our unwillingness to soberly address history, acknowledge systemic sin, reckon with our ancestors' sins, and answer Scripture's call to corporate responsibility leads us to forsake lament. Rah expounds, "Lament calls for an authentic encounter with the truth and challenges privilege, because privilege would hide the truth that creates discomfort."[16] He concludes, "The dismantling of privilege requires the disavowal of any pretense of exceptionalism."[17]

While lamentation is imperative, it must beget repentance to be redemptive. The problem, however, is that we have deluded ourselves into thinking oral confession is repentance. Saying "I am sorry" is not equivalent to turning away from sin. Confession of sin is only part of what turning back to God entails. We, like Israel before us, have conformed to the patterns of this world, embracing the love of money and rugged individualism in ways that bear false witness to the gospel of Jesus Christ.

Esther and Mordecai embodied the polarities of what Brueggemann describes when he writes, "If you eat the bread of Babylon for very long, you will be destroyed. Some like the bread of Babylon, and they become Babylonians; but Israelites who are exiles will not accommodate that imperial bread."[18] Esther, having become satiated by imperial bread, needed Mordecai's rejection of it to awaken her to the blindness privilege fosters. His lament could not be palatable because it had to cut through the imperial numbness to remind her of who she truly was and whose she was. His lament had to be unadulterated because it had to convict and convert Esther, helping her realize that God had not entrusted her with privilege as the queen for selfish indulgence but for the liberation of her people. Bearing witness to the prophetic power of public lament, Mordecai reminded Esther of the suffering of those beyond the comfortable confines of the palace. She was not actually Persian, despite her acculturation, and she had a unique opportunity to leverage her privilege for the furtherance of the kingdom and the good of her people.

Mordecai, who previously instructed Esther to conceal her Jewish identity, now told her she must reveal it. He also told Esther to break the law by making an unsolicited visit to see the king. Patriarchy made it illegal for Esther to see her husband without being beckoned. In fact, doing so could have resulted in her death. Recognizing this reality, plus recalling Queen Vashti's fate and being familiar with the king's temper, Esther balked at Mordecai's instructions.

For Such a Time as This

Mordecai passionately responded, "Do not think that because you are in the king's house you alone of all the Jews will escape. For if you remain silent at this time, relief and deliverance for the Jews will arise from another place, but you and your father's family will perish. And who knows but that you have come to your royal position for such a time as this?" (Est. 4:13–14). While Mordecai emphatically declared that being the king's wife would not save Esther if she chose not to act, he was also reminding her that God had strategically positioned her to alter the fate of her people. As queen she had unique access to influence the king—even amid this patriarchal structure—and to advocate for her people. While speaking up came at great personal risk for Esther—she could be put to death, jettisoned from the palace, or dethroned like Vashti—Mordecai helped her realize that declining this opportunity to leverage her privilege for justice would be selfish and unfaithful.

Choosing to speak out against evil will always cost us

something, and staying silent as oppression abounds will fatally seal the fate of our neighbors. While many have been taught to understand silence as neutrality or simply staying above the fray, silence amid oppression legitimates the status quo and only leads to more suffering, injustice, and death. In fact, Dr. Martin Luther King Jr. wrote, "He who passively accepts evil is as much involved in it as he who helps to perpetrate it. He who accepts evil without protesting against it is really cooperating with it."[19]

When faced with choosing self-preservation or sacrificial love, we must sit with Jesus' words: "Whoever wants to be my disciple must deny themselves and take up their cross and follow me. For whoever wants to save their life will lose it, but whoever loses their life for me will find it. What good will it be for someone to gain the whole world, yet forfeit their soul?" (Matt. 16:24–26). Choosing love in the face of fear is scary, and leveraging privilege for the furtherance of the kingdom and the good of our neighbor usually feels daunting—like Jesus' invitation to Peter to walk on water. While Jesus never promises bearing our cross daily will result in a happy ending—it did not for Queen Vashti—he does guarantee it is always worth it.

While happy endings are not promised, we know sacrificial love produces kingdom fruit and has the power to change the world. We have seen this through Jesus liberating us from the shackles of sin and death and disarming the powers and authorities through the cross, Moses leading Israel to freedom, and the good Samaritan embodying the Golden Rule[20] in biblical times. We've seen it through Harriet Tubman liberating enslaved people, Cesar Chavez and Dolores Huerta securing just working conditions and compensation for farmworkers through the United Farm Workers movement, and Father Greg Boyle creating transformative spaces for restoration, dignity, and vocation for former gang members and returning citizens in contemporary times.

When we choose sacrificial love amid injustice, Jesus accepts our humble offerings, blesses them, and multiplies them. Like with the fish and the loaves, Jesus can take even our meager offerings and transform them into profound expressions of love that have the capacity to transform lives, systems, and society. When we are meek enough to take on the mindset of Christ, not looking to our own interests but to the interests of others, we participate in the redemptive work of God. While pain is involved in this sacrifice, 1 Corinthians 15:58 reminds us to "stand firm. Let nothing move you. Always give yourselves fully to the work of the Lord, because you know that your labor in the Lord is not in vain."

Considering whether to leverage privilege for the furtherance of the kingdom and the good of our neighbor compels us to count the cost of discipleship anew. First John 2:15–17 reads, "Do not love the world or anything in the world. If anyone loves the world, love for the Father is not in them. For everything in the world—the lust of the flesh, the lust of the eyes, and the pride of life—comes not from the Father but from the world. The world and its desires pass away, but whoever does the will of God lives forever." We, like Esther, must decide if we want to save our lives rather than lose them for Jesus. Leveraging privilege for justice affords us the opportunity to prophetically bear witness to our commitment to seek God's kingdom and righteousness first, over and against the desires of this world.

Esther told Mordecai to gather all the Jews in Susa and have them join her and her attendants in a three-day fast. She then said, "When this is done, I will go to the king, even though it is against the law. And if I perish, I perish" (Est. 4:16). Brenda Salter McNeil writes, "When Esther decides she will take a stand for her people, the very first thing she chooses to do is pray. . . . Her first impulse is to acknowledge and seek God, and she calls on her community to do likewise."[21] The prayers of the people center Esther, affirming God's call on her life and empowering her to do what is necessary.

On the third day, Esther put on her royal robes and went before the king. When Xerxes saw Esther, he was pleased and held out his gold scepter to welcome her. Esther approached, and the king asked, "What is it, Queen Esther? What is your request? Even up to half the kingdom, it will be given you" (Est. 5:3). Esther, counterintuitively, replied by inviting the king and Haman to a banquet she had prepared for them. The king summoned Haman, and they went to Esther's banquet. As they were drinking wine and conversing, the king again asked Esther, "Now what is your petition? It will be given you. And what is your request? Even up to half the kingdom, it will be granted" (Est. 5:6). Esther implausibly replied by inviting the king and Haman to yet another banquet the next day. However, this time she ended her invitation by saying, "Then I will answer the king's question" (Est. 5:8).

Haman left the banquet drunk and encountered Mordecai—the insubordinate Jew who refused to bow before him again. Infuriated, Haman went home, summoned his friends and wife, boasted about his significance, and vented about Mordecai. They told Haman to have a pole erected and to ask the king to have Mordecai impaled on it. Haman heeded their advice and had the pole set up.

That evening, God troubled Xerxes's soul. Amid his insomnia, Xerxes was led by the Spirit to order the book of the chronicles—the record of his reign—to be brought in and read. The chronicles reminded Xerxes that Mordecai saved his life. Shortly after, Haman entered the court on his way to ask Xerxes to kill Mordecai.

> When Haman entered, the king asked him, "What should be done for the man the king delights to honor?"
>
> Now Haman thought to himself, "Who is there that the king would rather honor than me?" So he answered the king, "For the man the king delights to honor, have them bring a royal robe the king has worn and a horse the king has ridden, one with a royal crest placed on its head. Then let the robe and horse be entrusted to one of the king's most noble princes. Let them robe the man the king delights to honor, and lead him on the horse through the city streets, proclaiming before him, 'This is what is done for the man the king delights to honor!'"
>
> "Go at once," the king commanded Haman. "Get the robe and the horse and do just as you have suggested for Mordecai the Jew, who sits at the king's gate. Do not neglect anything you have recommended." (Est. 6:6–10)

Humiliated and defeated, Haman had to parade Mordecai throughout the city. Esther then revealed to Xerxes that she was Jewish and explained that Haman's decree meant that she, Mordecai, and every Jew in Persia must die. The king, enraged by Haman's actions, probably embarrassed by his complicity, and influenced by alcohol, ordered Haman to be impaled on the same pole he erected to kill Mordecai.

Esther and Mordecai worked with the king to terminate the Jewish genocide, and Jews throughout Persia celebrated God's sovereignty in a foreign land. As Brenda Salter McNeil explains, "Vashti's civil disobedience paved the way for Esther to enter into the story of God's healing and deliverance for the Jews. It was the courageous sacrifice of Vashti that called Esther forth. Had there not been a Vashti who stood up for herself, there would not have been an Esther."[22] Additionally, had there not been a Mordecai reminding Esther that her privilege had a redemptive purpose, her privilege would have actually been her demise, and God would have found another way to liberate the Jews. God's restoration is never dependent on us, but part of the good news of the gospel is that God invites us to partner in the work of restoration. When we chose to leverage privilege for the furtherance of the kingdom and the good of our neighbors, we become instruments of peace that God uniquely uses to induce freedom and justice for our fractured world.

Reflection Questions

1. How could discussing Queen Vashti's experience open up spaces for healing and restoration in churches?
2. How could your congregation start to address sexual violence?
3. How did the Persian Empire normalize the suppression of women's voices and autonomy? How does this happen today where you live?

4. Do you have a Mordecai in your life—a trusted voice who holds you accountable and reminds you to stay attuned to your neighbors' pain?

5. How can privilege blind us to oppression? And even after we recognize it, how can fear keep us silent about it?

6. What helped Esther choose to save her people over maintaining her individual privilege?

CHAPTER 4

MOSES

Leveraging Privilege to Birth Liberation

M oses became a Christian patriarch because of faithful women who feared God more than they feared Pharaoh. Their fear of God compelled them to follow the Spirit's lead to defy Pharaoh's direct order, break the law, save Moses' life, and subversively wield their wit to evade Pharaoh's wrath.

After the Hebrew midwives spared Moses' life, Jochebed, Miriam, and Pharaoh's daughter collaboratively raised, nurtured, and discipled him. They laid the faith foundation for one of the most righteous men to ever live and sowed seeds that would blossom into his faith-rooted activism. Despite holding divergent statuses within the Egyptian Empire—Jochebed and Miriam were disenfranchised, while Pharaoh's daughter epitomized privilege—these women shared an ethical commitment to act in the face of oppression, and they passed on this virtue to Moses. Yet Moses did not immediately embody this virtue, and when he began to, it took him awhile to hone and exercise it in productive ways.

Moses resided in the opulence of the palace—seemingly undisturbed by the oppression transpiring beyond the royal walls—until he was forty years old. Like Esther, satiation and insulation within the luxurious confines of the palace blinded Moses to the suffering of his people. His spiritual development was also stunted by an identity crisis. As a Hebrew raised within the imperial belly of the beast, Moses navigated double consciousness as he was coerced to assimilate into an Egyptian culture that was fiscally dependent on dehumanizing and exploiting the people to whom he ethnically belonged. W. E. B. Du Bois defined double consciousness as "this sense of always looking at one's self through the eyes of others, of measuring one's soul by the tape of a world that looks on in amused contempt and pity. One ever feels his two-ness, an American, a Negro; two souls, two thoughts, two unreconciled strivings; two warring ideals in one dark body, whose dogged strength alone keeps it from being torn asunder."[1] Moses, raised in Pharaoh's house, had to experience the two-ness of being Egyptian yet also a Hebrew.

Imagine Moses' cognitive dissonance, raised by the daughter of a man who crafted legislation intended to kill him upon his birth, while also being reared by his biological mom and sister who not only acted to save his life but were themselves tormented by the Egyptian Empire. Being raised within Pharaoh's house as a Hebrew must have been confounding, especially as Moses tried to discern who he was, where he belonged, and to whom he was authentically bound. Moses would carry the trauma of navigating "two warring ideals in one dark body," and it informed his decisions.

The heavy burden of navigating two warring ideals in a pigmented body is something BIPOC (Black, Indigenous, People of Color) leaders who work and minister in majority culture spaces know all too well. This heavy yoke wears on us, literally taking years off our lives and joy from our souls.[2] Under these circumstances, mental health feels elusive and self-care becomes requisite.

Black women, from Ida B. Wells to Fannie Lou Hamer, Pauli Murray, Audre Lord, and Chanequa Walker-Barnes, have led the way in naming this reality. Brenda Salter McNeil also recently addressed this reality by updating her "roadmap to reconciliation." In *Roadmap to Reconciliation 2.0*, McNeil writes,

> I have included the restoration cycle as a new aspect of the reconciliation process. As my understanding and application of this work have evolved, the Roadmap 2.0 model now reflects the need for people of color to have opportunities for restoration as a part of their reconciliation process. . . . The restoration process acknowledges that people of color are constantly doing the work of reconciliation and embodying the tension of living in a racialized society.[3]

Having a space for restoration is imperative for BIPOC leaders. It is the only way to sustain ourselves in the work we are called to. When we lead without tending to our souls and our racial trauma—in any space, be it a homogeneous space of color or a multiethnic space—we burn out, lead out of our shadow sides (our decentered selves), and draw from an empty well.

Nevertheless, the need for self-care, mental health, and restoration is amplified for BIPOC leaders working and ministering in white cultural spaces. Howard Thurman also addressed this need for restoration in his book *Deep Is the Hunger*, where he wrote about the lack of restorative resources for BIPOC leaders "who are intent upon establishing islands of fellowship in a sea of racial, religious, and national tensions."[4]

It is easy to lose your identity amid acculturating into an oppressive context that does not value where you come from, the people you belong to, or who you authentically are. This toxic environment prohibited Moses from discerning and heeding God's call upon his life. Consequently, the Spirit moved to disrupt Moses' contentment with palace living and inspired him to leave to reconnect with his own people. Moses, who had lived a sheltered life up until this point, was unprepared for the oppression and suffering he encountered among his sisters and brothers—who, in Egypt, constituted the least of these.

Trauma: Fight or Flight

Moses became overwhelmed by the barbarity and exploitation he witnessed while with his people. He was triggered by an Egyptian overseer ruthlessly beating a Hebrew. Moses instinctually intervened to interrupt the abuse, but his trauma overtook him. He surveyed the scene for witnesses and, seeing none, murdered the Egyptian in a trauma-informed response and buried his body. This was a manifestation of the age-old adage that "hurt people hurt people."

Traumatized people who do not address the root causes

of their trauma are overtaken by their trauma. Bessel van der Kolk, a noted psychiatrist who has won awards for his trauma research, addresses this phenomenon in the seminal text *The Body Keeps the Score*. Van der Kolk writes that "trauma compromises the brain," and explains that the destructive behavior of traumatized people is "not the result of moral failings or signs of lack of willpower or bad character—they are caused by actual changes to the brain"[5] trauma induces. Kolk expounds,

> We have learned that trauma is not just an event that took place sometime in the past; it is also the imprint left by that experience on mind, brain, and body. This imprint has ongoing consequences for how the human organism manages to survive in the present. Trauma results in a fundamental reorganization of the way mind and brain manage perceptions. It changes not only how we think and what we think about, but also our very capacity to think.[6]

Moses, who grew up in a context where Hebrews were constantly disparaged and subjugated, was retraumatized (a conscious or unconscious reminder of past trauma) witnessing his fellow Hebrew assaulted and found himself in fight-or-flight mode. Fight or flight is

> when traumatized people are presented with images, sounds, or threats related to their particular experience, the amygdala [what our brains depend on to warn us of impending danger and to activate our innate stress responses] reacts with alarm.... Activation of this fear center triggers the cascade of stress hormones and nerve impulses that drive up

blood pressure, heart rate, and oxygen intake—preparing the body for fight or flight.[7]

Moses fought, but his resistance did not further the kingdom. Since he had not tended to the root causes of his trauma, discerned God's call upon his life, or learned to hone his righteous indignation by channeling it for constructive change, he responded to imperial violence with violence.

The next day, Moses went back out among his people and discovered two Hebrews fighting. Having learned something from the previous day, he intervened again, but this time he assumed the posture of a peacemaker. He tried to reconcile the dispute by reminding the men that they were brothers, but the Hebrew instigating the scuffle pushed Moses, challenged his authority, and retorted, "Are you thinking of killing me as you killed the Egyptian?" (Ex. 2:14). Thinking no one had witnessed his crime, Moses was startled. He became afraid, worried about what would happen if word got out about the murder, and his fear was validated when Pharaoh heard of the crime. Pharaoh responded to the news by trying to kill Moses—again. Moses fled for his life, relocating in Midian.

Collective Liberation

While in Midian, Moses married Zipporah, started a family, and was discipled by Jethro, Zipporah's father and priest of Midian. One day while Moses was tending Jethro's flock, he encountered the angel of the Lord in a burning bush. As Moses investigated why the blazing bush was not consumed, God called Moses by name from within the bush. Moses responded by approaching the bush, and God told him to halt and remove his shoes because he was on holy ground. A conversation ensued, and God told Moses, "I have indeed seen the misery of my people in Egypt. I have heard them crying out because of their slave drivers, and I am concerned about their suffering. So I have come down to rescue them from the hand of the Egyptians" (Ex. 3:7–8). God then commissioned Moses to go to Pharaoh and lead the Israelites out of Egypt, explaining that he would serve as the conduit for divine liberation.

Imagine Moses' trepidation upon hearing God's plan. It had been forty years since Moses was last in Egypt, and he left fleeing for his life. Egypt had been a source of trauma, violence, and oppression for Moses. There he was separated from his biological family, was socialized into a culture that saw him as inferior, and witnessed his people brutalized, exploited, and enslaved. These traumatic experiences legitimated Moses' resistance to God's plan. Nevertheless, God called Moses to leave comfort and security yet again to reconnect with his people and to identify with their suffering. At forty years old, Moses was compelled by the Spirit to leave the palace, and then at eighty years old, he was commissioned by God to return to Egypt to confront Pharaoh. Moses' identity, purpose, and mission were fatefully tied to his people's condition, and though he seemed to escape this reality for seasons, God continued to bring him back to the oppression his people endured. God continued to remind Moses that he could not be truly free until his people were liberated.

God challenged Moses to reimagine freedom, to redefine it in a collective, rather than individualistic, manner. The Spirit troubled Moses' soul when he thought freedom was satiation in the palace as his people suffered beyond the royal walls. The

Spirit led him to reconnect to his people and opened his eyes to their suffering. However, since Moses was still on his own spiritual journey, he did not comprehend what God was up to. Then, after Moses had established a comfortable life in Midian with his family and was discipled by Jethro, God appeared again and disturbed his comfortable life once more. This time God revealed to Moses that divine liberation could not be authentically found in fugitive escape or in establishing geographic distance from the cries of one's people.

People from disenfranchised communities are often tempted to ascribe to this mirage of freedom when they leave the state for college, graduate, and settle down in the suburbs or begin to climb the corporate ladder. While each of these things are great, too many Christians—particularly in this context—succumb to thinking that when oppression is out of sight and out of mind, they are free. God corrected this line of thinking in Moses' life.

Being afforded an opportunity to leave home to gain skills, tools, and resources to better our lives is a privilege, but we must remain vigilant when we are afforded such opportunities. Satan will distort them and turn them into selfish, futile missions of trying to escape internalized oppression when you have come from a disenfranchised community where the people believe that nothing good can come. Shifting how we think about education can help us resist these impulses toward rugged individualism and internalized oppression. Our education is not solely for us as individuals. We receive an education so we can bring back our knowledge, skills, and resources to enrich and transform the communities that formed and shaped us.

Physically distancing ourselves from the pain of our people

and the suffering of our neighbors is a privilege. When we exploit our resources or talents to try to permanently escape the plight of our peers, we fail to faithfully steward our privilege. We join the imperial rat race instead of pursuing the kingdom on earth as it is in heaven. We forsake an opportunity to embrace shalom and become agents of transformation.

What we have been entrusted with is not just for us. The resources we possess have not been bestowed unto us just to create geographic distance for our families from the world's brokenness. We are blessed to be a blessing, to reinvest in our communities, and to contribute to communal flourishing. When we exploit our privilege to run away from the pain of our communities, we miss transformational opportunities to help induce freedom, liberation, and deliverance where captivity, disenfranchisement, and despair have reigned too long. We are not saviors, but the Spirit works through willing vessels who offer their lives to the Lord as living sacrifices, those who are intent on seeking the peace and prosperity of their communities because they know that flourishing occurs when the hood prospers.

Theologian Justo González writes about the collective freedom God was opening Moses up to. "Moses, after the encounter with the burning bush, goes back to his people for their liberation." González explains that Moses' encounters with God were not merely for his personal salvation but occurred "in order [for Moses] to go back to his people to do the work of God with and among them." González concludes that Scripture highlights "the importance of one's people for one's own religious obedience and fulfillment."[8] This new vision of freedom called Moses into solidarity with suffering and challenged him to realize what Maya Angelou would later prophetically declare: "The truth is, no one of us can be free until everybody is free."[9]

Dr. King, in his iconic "Letter from a Birmingham Jail," also unpacked what this kingdom vision of mutuality and collective liberation entails: "I am cognizant of the interrelatedness of all communities and states. I cannot sit idly by in Atlanta and not be concerned about what happens in Birmingham. Injustice anywhere is a threat to justice everywhere. We are caught in an inescapable network of mutuality, tied in a single garment of destiny. Whatever affects one directly, affects all indirectly."[10] King then concluded, "We know through painful experience that freedom is never voluntarily given by the oppressor; it must be demanded by the oppressed."[11] Dr. King's vision of militant, nonviolent, civil disobedience was undoubtedly informed by Moses' leadership and the book of Exodus.

Confronting Pharaoh

Confronting Pharaoh is unnerving because ministry to dismantle imperial oppression is met with resistance from principalities, powers, rulers of the darkness of this world, and spiritual wickedness in high places. When God sends you to confront Pharaoh and uproot imperial oppression, the empire will try to crucify you, and you literally will have to offer your body as a living sacrifice to the Lord. Defying the powers that be requires a resolute belief that God truly is the great "I Am." W. E. B. Du Bois articulates the questions one must consider before following the Spirit's lead to confront Pharaoh: "How shall Integrity face Oppression? What shall Honesty do in the face of Deception, Decency in the face of Insult, Self-Defense before Blows? How shall Desert and Accomplishment meet Despising, Detraction, and Lies? What shall Virtue do to meet Brute Force?" Du Bois then explains, "There are so many answers and so contradictory; and such differences for those on the one hand who meet questions similar to this once a year or once a decade, and those who face them hourly and daily."[12]

Moses is an intriguing person to apply Du Bois's questions to because he ethnically belonged to a people who faced these questions daily, but he was privileged and raised in the palace where he may have been confronted with these questions once a decade. Then he relocated to Midian where he may have been confronted with them once a year. In this way, Moses represents privileged BIPOC individuals who are able to escape the weight of oppression—because of their class, education, geographic location, or vocation—in which most of their peers are mired.

Privileged BIPOC who are not connected to the pain of their people face a unique challenge when the Spirit disrupts their comfort, reveals to them that they are not free, and prompts them to reconnect with their people and identify with their suffering. These individuals are applauded by most for "escaping" and are lauded as exceptional—manifestations of the American dream and examples of what is possible when rugged individualism is undergirded by personal accountability. They are upheld by majority culture, politicians, and institutions to deny, deflect, and trivialize the deathly realities of systemic sin and institutional racism their disenfranchised people bemoan. They, like Moses, really do believe that they are free, and the last thing they want to do is go back to Egypt or stand in solidarity with their oppressed people, much less confront Pharaoh.

Sometimes we are called to leverage our privilege to further the kingdom and love our neighbor, and other times we must abandon it altogether. In leaving the palace and Midian to confront Pharaoh, Moses demonstrated that God calls us to forsake privilege when it inhibits our witness and prevents us from responding to the cries of agony that arise from our people's oppression. As Archbishop Óscar Romero said, "When the church hears the cry of the oppressed it cannot but denounce the social structures that give rise to and perpetuate the misery from which the cry arises."[13] Moses forsook his privilege and returned to his people, joined with his siblings, and led them into liberation. The site of resistance was at the place of marginalization. God summoned Moses to protest imperial oppression and empowered him to lead a movement of militant, nonviolent, civil disobedience that became the archetype of righteous resistance throughout time.

Protest must disrupt the oppressive status quo, expose evil, and dismantle the structures that stabilize it. The God-inspired civil disobedience Moses led elucidates that even Spirit-led resistance movements where protestors are nonviolent have injurious outcomes. Waging peace amid oppression is convoluted and nuanced. The protest God called Moses to lead and directed him through destabilized Egypt's economy— which was rooted in oppression—resulting in property damage and the destruction of natural resources. Moreover, because of Pharaoh's hardened heart and the disobedience of Egypt, the plagues caused death, with the firstborn Egyptian sons being killed. While damage, devastation, and death are certainly not God's original intent, this passage shows that they may be consequences for societies built on injustice, repression, and sin. In tyrannical contexts, God will induce liberation by any means necessary, and Scripture shows that the great I Am frequently chooses to use flawed but faithful leaders like Moses as instruments of divine peace to end systemic sin and oppression.

Do not misconstrue God's liberating action to end systemic sin and oppression as a promotion of looting, rioting, or arson, but rather understand it as an explanation illuminating that Scripture reveals that a society built on oppression and injustice will not stand. Unjust societies will crumble by God's hand. And divine deconstruction will not always occur in ways that we recognize as God's hand and may not manifest in ways we are comfortable with. A clear difference exists though between God's supernatural acts that cause destruction and damage that is caused by belligerent anarchists or fatalistic dissenters. But the exodus clearly illustrates that when God calls a leader to resist evil and they follow the Spirit's lead, property destruction may very well be part of God's restorative justice.

Bearing a faithful witness amid protest to end imperial oppression is challenging. State-sanctioned violence can tempt those who endure it to sin, as we saw when Moses killed the Egyptian. Nevertheless, we cannot allow fear of this possibility to immobilize us and cause us to stand idly by and allow imperial oppression to transpire uninterruptedly on our watch. Theologian Willie Jennings—after the murder of George Floyd by Officer Derek Chauvin—spoke to the complexity of resisting state-sanctioned violence while faithfully bearing witness to our new life in Christ. In an interview, Jennings said,

> God wants us to hate what God hates. God invites us into a
> shared fury, but only the kind that we creatures can handle.
> You all know that anger is frightening because it is not easily

controllable. Anger can easily touch hatred, and if anger enters into hatred, then we will be drawn into violence, and way too many people in this world have been drawn deeply into violence. What Christian faith knows is that the way to keep anger from hatred is not to deny anger, to pretend that it is not real. No, we cannot do that. What keeps anger from touching hatred is not the cunning of reason or the power of will. It is simply Jesus.

For the Christian, Jesus stands between anger and hatred, prohibiting the reach, blocking the touch and saying to us, "Don't go there. There is nothing there but death." Anger, bound to God's righteous indignation has a different purpose for us. It points us to the change that must happen, that is the overturning of an unjust world order.[14]

Jesus is at work in protest movements, keeping Christians who publicly resist evil rooted in God's love and prohibiting our righteous indignation from touching hatred. Jesus is what sustained the prophetic witness of Howard Thurman, Óscar Romero, and Ella Baker amid their resistance to tyranny and rooted them in love and a commitment to nonviolence amid being persecuted and brutalized. Jesus is what empowered Dr. Martin Luther King Jr. to declare, "Yes, it is love that will save our world and our civilization, love even for enemies,"[15] during the civil rights movement when he was incarcerated twenty-nine times, bludgeoned and targeted for proclaiming the gospel and functioning as an ambassador of reconciliation. Each of these leaders took their cues from Moses, who was willing to abandon his privilege to fulfill God's call on his life, liberating his people and furthering the kingdom.

Moses, like the women who raised him, learned to con-structively act in the face of oppression and fear, channeling his righteous indignation into kingdom change. He, too, embodied a self-giving ethic of belonging to those whom he was socialized within the palace to see as disconnected from him, as inferior to him. He, too, put his life on the line, opposing Pharaoh to fight for justice, pursue freedom, and stand in solidarity with those he had the "privilege" of ignoring. God compelled Moses to reexamine his life and all that he had been entrusted with. Moses came to realize that he was blessed to be a blessing, that he had a responsibility to use his access to the "master's tools" to dismantle Pharaoh's oppressive house. God moved Moses from apathy to activism—to the point where he was willing not only to leverage his privilege but to forsake the pleasures and prestige of the palace, to sojourn in solidarity with the oppressed into the desert for righteousness' sake.

Hebrews 11 articulates the role faith played in Moses' for-mation and witness.

By faith Moses' parents hid him for three months after he was born, because they saw he was no ordinary child, and they were not afraid of the king's edict.

By faith Moses, when he had grown up, refused to be known as the son of Pharaoh's daughter. He chose to be mis-treated along with the people of God rather than to enjoy the fleeting pleasures of sin. He regarded disgrace for the sake of Christ as of greater value than the treasures of Egypt, because he was looking ahead to his reward. By faith he left Egypt, not fearing the king's anger; he persevered because he saw him who is invisible. By faith he kept the Passover and the application of blood, so that the destroyer of the firstborn would not touch the firstborn of Israel.

By faith the people passed through the Red Sea as on dry land; but when the Egyptians tried to do so, they were drowned. (vv. 23–29)

One of the most challenging passages in Scripture is 2 Corinthians 5:7, which calls us to walk by faith and not by sight—especially when living in despotic context. This is because, as humans, we are prone to walk by sight, allowing what we see to dictate what we believe and how we live. To believe that God is good, sovereign, and active amid oppression is challenging. We are prone to doubt, question, and wonder if God's promises are true when our communities continue to be decimated by state-sanctioned violence and systemic sin. When we walk by sight, we believe that death has the final word, and injustice will ultimately reign. Nevertheless, we must be acutely aware of the consequences of allowing our sight to order our steps and dictate our witness. When sight usurps faith, dissonance erodes into hopelessness, resistance becomes vengeance, and we ultimately have an identity crisis. We forget who we are and whose we are. We, like Moses, are called not to try to resist evil in our own power, for we are empowered by God and directed by the Spirit.

Moses was a flawed leader, and his deficiencies endear us to him. We connect with his identity crisis, quest for belonging, racial and ethnic trauma, and imperfect response to oppression. These struggles make him uniquely approachable as a biblical leader. He has a criminal background, comes from a "subordinate people" who were deemed disposable, was separated from his family due to systemic sin, and was forced to flee his home because of the threat of violence. As Moses fled Egypt to evade Pharaoh's ire, he was also—unbeknownst to him—setting off on a spiritual journey to find his identity, mission, and purpose.

Moses, like many of us, was not just full of doubts but had legitimate reasons why God should have chosen another, more competent leader to confront Pharaoh. Nevertheless, God insisted that liberating Israel was Moses' calling and purpose. God assured Moses that in spite of his insecurities, not only did he have everything he needed to fulfill his task, but the "Great I Am" would be with him throughout the mission.

God is a waymaker who directed Moses' path, protecting him from infanticide and granting him refuge within the heart of an oppressive empire; reunifying his family after systemic sin separated them; leading him out of the cloistered life of the palace to reconnect him with his people; opening his eyes to the oppression and exploitation the Hebrews endured; and leading him to Midian where he started a family and was discipled and spiritually groomed to faithfully lead. God directed Moses' steps and used every piece of Moses' story, including his ethnic trauma and the dysfunction it caused—the murder of the Egyptian—to prepare him for this divinely inspired campaign of militant, non-violent civil disobedience. God hears the cries of the oppressed and chooses to work through insecure, flawed people like Moses to induce freedom.

Sacrificing Individual Freedom to Pursue Collective Liberation

As God did for Moses, God transformed the life of my friend and colleague Jonathan Brooks (Pastah J) by bringing him back to a place to which he never wanted to return. In his book *Church Forsaken*, Pastah J talks about growing up in West Englewood, one of the most stigmatized neighborhoods on the south side of Chicago—and the entire US. In 2018 more than 40 percent of families in Englewood lived below the poverty line, and there were fifty homicides.[16] Englewood has become a common talking point for politicians who pathologize Black families and communities and ask questions like, "If black lives matter, then why do Black people refuse to protest gun violence in their own communities?"

Pastah J, after describing a shooting in his community, wrote,

> I was once a young man who was itching to get as far as possible from my neighborhood. I traveled to Tuskegee University in Alabama for college, with the hope of never returning to Chicago. If I did return, it would not be to the same economic situation or neighborhood. I studied architecture rather than art or music because I needed to be confident that I could move the economic class needle forward for my family. Where I ended up economically and geographically at the end of this journey was paramount to my understanding of success. Now, twenty years later, as an unplanned return resident, I love Englewood passionately and couldn't imagine living anywhere else.[17]

God brought Pastah J back to Englewood to take over Canaan Community Church at the ripe age of twenty-six. He had other plans, but the Spirit of God would not relent. God did not bring Pastah J back to Englewood just to lead the members of his church, however; God used the pain of the Englewood community to change Pastah J and in turn used him to move the Englewood community toward a collectivist vision of liberation, with a new sense of pride, dignity, and value in themselves and their neighborhood.

Pastah J has become an integral leader not just in the Englewood neighborhood but in the city of Chicago. He has received numerous awards for his civic engagement and economic and community development. Pastah J was named the "Hometown Hero" by Chicago Defender Charities, asked to serve as the marshal for the 2017 Bud Billiken Parade, and awarded the Traditioned Innovation Award from Duke Divinity and *Faith & Leadership* magazine in 2019. His church runs Canaan Community Redevelopment Corporation and Five Loaves Food Co-Op to increase healthy food options for neighbors.

Pastah J played a vital role in bringing a Whole Foods Market into Englewood, which was previously a food desert. Pastah J, however, knew that a traditional Whole Foods would not work in Englewood, given the chain's high food prices and the community's high poverty rates. He participated in an Englewood delegation who negotiated with Whole Foods to get the franchise to agree that if a Whole Foods came to Englewood, the grocery store chain would reduce its prices on staples such as milk and bread compared to other Whole Foods locations. It would be committed to hiring community residents and offering them health insurance, intentionally making shelf space for products from local vendors, and designing the interior of the store in a way that would reflect the spirit of the community.

Pastah J admits to having reservations about entering into negotiations with Whole Foods. He said, "I had pegged them"[18] as gentrifiers, a chain that was not humble enough to work with the needs of our community. "The very thing I hate, my neighborhood being defined by an outside narrative versus a real relationship—I did the same thing to Whole Foods. And they showed me that, no, they care about people, not just profits. I saw it with my own eyes."[19] So, because of leaders like Pastah J and the Whole Foods leadership's authentic desire and willingness to work with Englewood leaders, the Englewood Whole Foods opened at 63rd and Halsted in 2016. Since then, other businesses have opened within Englewood, including a Starbucks, which has also committed to hiring community members and giving them benefits.

In addition to helping bring economic development to Englewood, Pastah J has consistently participated in and orchestrated night walks in Englewood and nearby neighborhoods to decrease crime, drug activity, and gun violence. He and other leaders have strategically identified hot spots throughout Chicago and have intentionally thrown community events and block parties when the block is hottest to cultivate communion, communal pride, and safety in the exact places and spaces where death, destruction, and violence have proven most likely to occur.

Pastah J and other pastors like him who have been prodded by the Spirit of God to return to their communities—where they may not have wanted to return—illustrate a Christlike posture in how they faithfully listen to the pain of the people, are transformed by their pain, and are intent on reimmersing themselves within this pain. They then mobilize the untapped potential of their communities and restore the vision of the residents by reminding them of how God, rather than the empire, sees them.

These pastors remind residents that the best news the world has ever known (Jesus) came from a ghetto (Nazareth) that no one believed anything good could come from.

Reflection Questions

1. Moses' faith foundation was laid by three powerful women. How have women informed your faith journey?
2. How has trauma impacted your life or the life of someone close to you?
3. Have you ever let your imperfections keep you from heeding God's call on your life?
4. How do we muster the courage to confront pharaohs? What is at risk if we do not confront pharaohs?
5. In a world that influences us to do otherwise, how does the gospel empower us to choose collective over individual freedom?
6. How is God calling you to leverage or abandon your privilege by faith?

CHAPTER 5

PAUL AND SILAS

*Leveraging Privilege to
Create Systemic Change*

Naming privilege requires spiritual maturity. It feels threatening because it reveals our sustained complicity with broken systems, structures, and laws that deface the *imago Dei* inherent in our neighbor. Despite the risk, the church must be courageous enough to address privilege because it distorts the communion God intends for us to enjoy with our Creator and with one another. Denying that privilege exists only exacerbates the evil it produces and prohibits us from actively participating as colaborers with Christ in reconciling the world to God.

Addressing privilege is only controversial because some who benefit from it are adamant about denying its existence. Some of these individuals renounce privilege on theological grounds, claiming the concept is unbiblical. Others contest it based on principles of individualism, refusing to apologize, take responsibility, or strive to make amends for "something I did not do" or "the sins of my ancestors." Still others reject the existence of privilege because they believe it insinuates that "I did not earn what I have through hard work." This chapter addresses these rebuttals and, more importantly, illustrates how refusing to acknowledge privilege leads to blindness and hardened hearts that embolden injustice.

Having privilege is not a sin, though privilege emerges from sin. What is sinful is exploiting privilege for our own advantage and turning a blind eye to the suffering of our neighbors in order to sustain it. Scripture repeatedly acknowledges privilege and provides insight into how privilege insidiously functions today. Learning to unmask privilege can be painful work, but the cure for the pain is in the pain. By candidly addressing privilege, we create a unique opportunity for the body of Christ to turn away from sin and reorient ourselves toward God and neighbor through the spiritual disciplines of remembrance, confession, lament, and repentance.

Taking this humble posture allows us to see that Scripture outlines how we faithfully steward privilege. The Bible gives us tangible tools to move beyond denying or feeling immobilized by privilege. Passages like Acts 16 elucidate how we can subversively leverage privilege to seek the kingdom first and become a cruciform people who sacrificially bear witness to the love of God in a broken world.

Solidarity as Sacrificial Love

Acts 16:16–40 is a story about police brutality, a corrupt criminal judicial system that is more committed to money than justice, and devout disciples who refuse to turn a blind eye to injustice within their midst. This passage exposes privilege, particularly in the last five verses. After Paul and Silas endured public persecution and humiliation—being stripped naked, beaten with rods, and severely flogged—they were falsely accused of crimes, stigmatized as Jewish foreigners, and unjustly imprisoned without even being given a trial. The text tells what happened the next morning:

> When it was daylight, the magistrates sent their officers to the jailer with the order: "Release those men." The jailer told Paul, "The magistrates have ordered that you and Silas be released. Now you can leave. Go in peace."
>
> But Paul said to the officers: "They beat us publicly without a trial, even though we are Roman citizens, and threw us into prison. And now do they want to get rid of us quietly? No! Let them come themselves and escort us out."
>
> The officers reported this to the magistrates, and when they heard that Paul and Silas were Roman citizens, they were alarmed. They came to appease them and escorted them from the prison, requesting them to leave the city. (Acts 16:35–39)

The magistrates only cared about their abuse of Paul and Silas when they realized they were Roman citizens. This is privilege. Privilege aborts justice, leading judicial systems, power structures, and governments to treat a person or group preferentially—with more compassion and dignity than others—because of their citizenship, class, surname, social capital, sexual orientation, religion, or an aspect of their embodiment (race, gender, ethnicity, able-bodiedness, attractiveness, and more). Judicially, privilege leads to unjust verdicts and societal outcomes that exacerbate the preexisting gaps between the privileged and the disenfranchised. Justice systems render these oppressive judicial decisions without ever truly being held accountable for the social inequities they produce and reinforce. This unethical judicial legacy is alive and well today in the US. As Bryan Stevenson explains, "We have a system of justice that treats you better if you're rich and guilty than if you're poor and innocent." He says, "Wealth—not culpability—shapes outcomes."[1]

Paul understood that he and Silas were denied access to a trial and were persecuted because they were misidentified as men without Roman citizenship. As Roman citizens, Paul and Silas were not surprised by the anti-Semitism inherent in Rome's judiciary. This implies that they had previously witnessed how the prejudice, bias, and ethnocentrism of Roman magistrates undermined justice.

Paul's response to the jailer further demonstrated his understanding of Rome's unjust judicial system. He knew exactly how to counter the immoral magistrates' attempt to conceal their oppression. Instead of allowing the Roman officials to sneak them out at the crack of dawn without witnesses, Paul demanded judicial accountability. He proclaimed to the jailer, "They beat us publicly without a trial, even though we are Roman citizens, and threw us into prison. And now do they want to get rid of us quietly? No! Let them come themselves and escort us out" (v. 37).

Since Paul knew that he and Silas were bludgeoned, denied a trial, and unjustly imprisoned because they were accused of being Jews, he also understood that he could have ended their oppression at any point by simply declaring that they were

Roman citizens. However, rather than exploiting their privilege to avoid suffering, Paul and Silas chose to endure persecution as "foreigners" in their hometown. They suffered in solidarity with the oppressed to expose the systemic sin the Roman criminal justice system was mired in. Paul and Silas thereby embodied the Christ hymn found in Philippians 2 by choosing to suffer in solidarity with those who did not have Roman citizenship, taking on the oppression that their non-Roman neighbors were subjected to daily.

Paul and Silas did this not because they created the problem but because they understood that non-Romans, particularly Jews, lacked the power and influence in Rome that was needed to unmask, overturn, and transform an oppressive judicial system. This was heavy lifting that only insiders—Romans, people of privilege—could do. Subsequently, they owned the responsibility of addressing the cancerous effects of privilege, even though they did not create the problem. They refused to walk away and consider their hands clean just because they were not the ones who created the biased system or enacted judicial oppression. They knew these individualistic approaches were not aligned with the cruciform ethic of Christ.

Paul and Silas demonstrated that when followers of Jesus notice injustice, we have a responsibility to intervene and work to end it, whether we helped create the injustice or not. Paul and Silas confronted a sin their country's foreparents were responsible for, a sin that they as Roman citizens were still benefiting from. However, rather than exploit these benefits for selfish gain, they subversively used them to bear witness to their true citizenship as followers of Christ.

Paul and Silas realized that as followers of Christ they were complicit if they knew that people without Roman citizenship, particularly Jews, were merely cannon fodder for an unjust criminal justice system yet did nothing to address this systemic problem. They also realized that it would have been unfaithful to exploit their privilege of citizenship to opt out of the persecution their neighbors without Roman citizenship were subjected to whenever they got ensnared in Rome's justice system. True solidarity requires suffering with, entering in when privilege tempts us to believe that we do not have to.

These disciples demonstrated a gospel-rooted understanding of solidarity. They embodied 1 Corinthians 1:18, which reminds us, "For the message of the cross is foolishness to those who are perishing, but to us who are being saved it is the power of God." Their sacrificial choice to suffer in solidarity with non-Romans made no sense to their fellow Roman citizens, and I am sure it made many of their peers question their patriotism.

Paul and Silas prophetically demonstrated that privilege is something Christians are called to steward, not exploit for selfish gain. Privilege, then, becomes a revolutionary tool that those who possess it are commissioned to leverage to hold corrupt systems and structures accountable and to forge systemic transformation that they know those without the same privilege, access, and social currency are unable to wield. Privilege therefore should not immobilize those who possess it but should embolden them to consider how they can subversively leverage it for the sake of righteousness. Exploring this understanding of privilege further, Willie Jennings writes,

> Paul will not keep silent. An injustice has been done against him and Silas, and they will not go quietly into freedom,

relieved that their ordeal is over. More is at stake than their freedom. This is a matter of justice. Paul and Silas are acting as disciples precisely in claiming their rights as citizens. Disciples are positioned against this political power of the secret. That power seeks to isolate and individuate injustices done, turning them into singular, episodic events that do not point to systemic, structural, and serial realities of oppression and the misuse of power. These disciples call out such operations, and they will use whatever resources of the nation state to do so. Roman citizenship will be used for the sake of another identity—a disciple of Jesus.[2]

After suffering in solidarity with immigrants and foreigners who had no citizenship in Rome, Paul and Silas declared their Roman citizenship to demand judicial accountability by forcing Roman magistrates to publicly acknowledge their corruption. As followers of Christ, they could not be content knowing that the justice system was just for Roman citizens and not for all people. This passage challenges Christians to develop eyes to see the injustices around us and to learn how we can intervene on behalf of our oppressed neighbors, suffer with them when necessary, and leverage our privilege to uproot oppression in our midst. Paul and Silas illustrate that we must employ privilege as an instrument to pursue justice and further the kingdom instead of denying its existence or feeling incapacitated by it.

We are commissioned to exercise our citizenship—and the privileges it affords—as a tool to create a more equitable society where all can flourish. Willie Jennings asserts that citizenship offers us a unique opportunity to sacrificially love our neighbors—particularly the least of these who are most afflicted by systemic sin. He writes,

> Disciples of Jesus should be desperate citizens. The desperate citizen will press their citizenship as far as possible for the sake of thwarting death and its agents. Paul, as he moves through the political ecology of Rome, illuminates this kind of citizenship. It is a citizenship that takes seriously the position of those most disadvantaged by empire, those trapped in the prisons, found begging on the streets, those receiving the brunt of its unleashed violence, and those made slaves to its economic machinations.[3]

However, rather than embracing this understanding, we too often view citizenship merely as something that guarantees us individual rights, freedoms, and liberties.

Jennings, like Paul and Silas in this passage, presses us to reimagine citizenship and how it can be used to pursue collective liberation rather than individual freedoms as we seek the kingdom first. Citizenship grants power, and how we use this power bears witness to where our allegiance lies. Kingdom citizens sacrificially use their citizenship to seek the peace and prosperity of their communities, to expose and address systemic sin, as well as to care for and dignify the least of these.

Understanding the power citizenship endowed, Paul and Silas recognized and seized the opportunity to wield their power politically, engaging in advocacy to create judicial accountability, reform, and transparency. Pursuing right(eous) relationship with God and neighbor not only requires Christians to understand the relationship between privilege and power but entails actualizing, exercising, and mobilizing the power that privilege affords us to leverage it for needed social change.

Politics are not salvific. Our hopes and dreams cannot become wed to politicians, partisanship, or outcomes, and we must remember that our two-party system is incapable of bringing kingdom transformation. Nevertheless, politics do offer us a unique opportunity to express tangibly our love of neighbor by addressing systemic injustice, generational sins, and governmental abuse of power.

While appropriately celebrating Paul and Silas for their subversive use of privilege, Willie Jennings fittingly cautions us to not misunderstand "this strategic use of citizenship as the approval of aspirations toward citizenship as the necessary path to freedom."[4] Because, as Jennings goes on to explain,

> The church has always been tempted to confuse citizenship with discipleship. The citizen who is a disciple can no longer be a citizen in the abstract, no longer a citizen in theory but only in the concrete practice of discipleship. The disciple is a citizen who has their citizenship tightly bound to the body of Jesus and ordered by the Spirit of God toward one purpose—to expose the concealed architecture of oppression and violence and to set the captives free.[5]

Paul and Silas—like Rev. James Reeb, Viola Liuzzo, Joan Trumpauer Mulholland, and Rev. Bruce Klunder, martyrs who gave their lives to stand in solidarity with their oppressed Black sisters and brothers during the civil rights era—understood the cost of discipleship, which led them to access the power and privilege they possessed to stand in solidarity with people to whom they were taught they were superior, and subversively leverage these tools for the kingdom and neighbors' good. These disciples of Christ chose the narrow road to produce fruit in keeping with repentance, even though this meant enduring persecution and sharing in Christ's sufferings in order to also share in his glory.

Proximity Changes Things

Bryan Stevenson, like the apostle Paul, noticed how an unjust criminal justice system was targeting and inequitably sentencing BIPOC in the United States. He, too, realized that his faith not only called him to identify the problem but to work to fix it. Stevenson chose to use his privilege, education, and social capital as a graduate of Harvard Law School to provide legal defense for the least of these in a judicial sense—those awaiting execution on death row without legal representation or without adequate legal representation. No one else wanted to touch most of the cases Stevenson zealously took on. In his relentless pursuit of truth and justice, Stevenson created the Equal Justice Initiative (EJI), which has fought for the dignity of disenfranchised incarcerated individuals for the past thirty-one years. Stevenson's unrelenting commitment to holding the US legal system accountable to its purpose of "equal justice under the law" led Archbishop Desmond Tutu to knight Stevenson as "America's Nelson Mandela" and has enabled EJI to successfully challenge more than 125 death row convictions.

I had the privilege of interviewing Stevenson about the debut of the film *Just Mercy*, which was adapted from his book of the same name. The film tells the story of Stevenson's faith-rooted activism. I asked him why, as a Harvard Law School graduate with a multitude of lucrative vocational options, he decided to dedicate his life to representing individuals most people and most lawyers have forsaken. He told me that living into Jesus' commission in Matthew 25 to visit those in prison changed everything for him, creating relationships and proximity where the Spirit moved. Stevenson explained that seeing firsthand what men and women on death row endured animated his faith and transformed his understanding of vocation.

> When I met people on death row who were literally dying for legal assistance. When I heard a condemned man sing about higher ground as we have in the film, everything just came together for me. My great-grandparents were enslaved. My grandmother survived lynching and terrorism. My parents were humiliated every day by Jim Crow laws that were designed to denigrate. And yet they had enough faith, they had enough hope, to love one another and to create another generation. And I want to honor that hope and that love and employ that same faith to believe that we can create something better for the people who come after. I do think there's something better waiting for us in this country. I do think there's something that feels more like freedom than inequality of justice. But to get there we're going to have to talk more honestly, we're going to have to work harder, we're going to have to do the difficult things that are sometimes required to love mercy and to do justice and to walk humbly with God.[6]

Two of the most difficult things we will have to learn to do are talk frankly about privilege and the oppression it sustains, and learn how to strategically leverage privilege—and the access and power it affords—for justice instead of exploiting it for selfish gain. Stevenson closed our interview with a call to action. I asked him what he hoped the film would inspire the church to do. He responded,

> I want to see people of faith get reengaged. The Gospels talk about not only feeding the hungry and clothing the naked and providing shelter to the homeless, but also about going into the jails and prisons and standing with the accused. And we haven't done that in a way that I think we should be. And I hope it still inspires a conversation that leads us into that place.[7]

As for Stevenson, the time my wife and I have spent behind bars has animated our faith. It has exposed our privilege in new ways and provoked us to try to follow Paul and Silas's example. I am blessed to have the opportunity to teach in a maximum-security prison. The program I teach in, which my wife is a part of as a free student, is the only program in the state of Illinois offering incarcerated individuals an opportunity to earn their master's degree. This is important because access to higher education behind bars has proven to be the most effective and fiscally responsible way to address recidivism.

As we have done life with our brothers behind bars, our commitment to ending mass incarceration has intensified. As we work for systemic change, we are assisting those in need in a tangible way. My wife, because of the power of proximity and the relationships she has developed with our brothers and sisters behind bars, decided that our first house had to be a duplex where we lived in one unit and used the second unit for transitional housing for returning citizens. She is also dreaming of creating a business that focuses on employing returning citizens, because the two biggest factors that lead people back behind bars once they are freed are an inability to secure long-term housing and securing employment that pays a livable wage. I share this as a small example of what leveraging privilege for the furtherance of the kingdom and the good of our neighbors could look like.

I am using my education privilege to invest in men who mostly came from communities that were socially divested. I am furthering the kingdom by discipling brothers in the faith and reminding them that they are not forever defined by the worst thing they have ever done, that they are loved by the Lord, and that God still has a missional purpose for their lives. Our family is leveraging our financial privilege by providing housing on a sliding scale, allowing returning citizens to get back on their feet, save some money, build some communal networks, and leave our housing program with an improved credit score and a good reference. No, this in and of itself does not change the system, but as we work for systemic change, we are also called to tend to the direct needs before us. We do not do this to be saviors or to try to earn salvation; we do this because we are called to love our neighbors sacrificially and to steward what we have been entrusted with to extend the compassion, mercy, and love that Christ first extended to us.

Reflection Questions

1. How does this passage (Acts 16:16–40) help you define and understand privilege?

2. What privileges are connected to citizenship?

3. Why was it important for Paul and Silas to endure what people without Roman citizenship had to endure on a daily basis?

4. Have you ever suffered in solidarity with your neighbors to bear witness to your faith in Jesus Christ?

5. How could you leverage your privilege to create systemic accountability and change?

6. How can you leverage your privilege and influence to help reform and deconstruct our criminal justice system, which is also riddled with biases?

CHAPTER 6

JESUS

Abandoning and Leveraging Privilege to Proclaim the Good News

Shortly before enduring the cross, Jesus gave his followers a new commandment, an identity marker that signifies to the world that we are his disciples: "A new command I give you: Love one another. As I have loved you, so you must love one another. By this everyone will know that you are my disciples, if you love one another" (John 13:34–35). As we unpack Jesus' command, we must pause and reflect on the "if" within it. We have free will. God does not force us to do anything, including love our neighbor. Therefore love is a choice, not a given. Love is an inconvenient choice, one that costs us time, resources, and at times our safety. God's love, empowered by the Spirit, compels us to be countercultural, bearing witness to who and whose we are through how we see, interact with, and affirm the *imago Dei* in all our neighbors.

First John 3:16 reveals, "This is how we know what love is: Jesus Christ laid down his life for us. And we ought to lay down our lives for our brothers and sisters." This verse is not metaphorical; it calls us to redefine love based on our Savior's example. Love is thus more than affinity or sentimentality. Christians are to define love as cruciform (reflective of the self-giving love displayed for us by Jesus on the cross), others oriented, and sacrificial in nature. Love calls us out of our comfort zones and into the pain our neighbors endure. Love means risking our lives for others, the way the midwives did for Moses and Esther and Moses did for their people. They could have chosen their individual safety and security, they could have just done what they were told and washed their hands of the suffering doing so would have caused, but the Spirit of the Lord compelled them to faithfulness through love.

In the verses that follow 1 John 3:16, we see that there are also material implications for love. Verses 17 and 18 read, "If anyone has material possessions and sees a brother or sister in need but has no pity on them, how can the love of God be in that person? Dear children, let us not love with words or speech but with actions and in truth." This passage illuminates that the love of God cannot exist in our hearts and minds alone; it must translate into tangible action. How we live out our faith, demonstrating the love of God when we see neighbors in need, bears witness to the world that God's love has transformed us into new creations. Furthermore, our ability to connect the excess in our lives to the lack in our neighbors' lives attests to our new life in Christ. Our faith therefore informs how we see and respond to brokenness around us. It informs our response to the needs of the least of these, especially those disenfranchised by imperial oppression.

The Material Cost of Discipleship

Few interactions illustrate the material cost of discipleship like Jesus' interaction with the rich young ruler in Matthew 19:16–22. This young man thought religion was about getting into heaven. He approached Jesus to ensure that he was good enough and had done enough to secure eternal life. He coveted Jesus' affirmation but only to assuage his doubts. This self-centered interaction was about uncovering any fine print he may have missed—and confirming that following Christ would not be too disruptive to his privileged lifestyle.

Jesus did not deny that the man had indeed obeyed all the commandments since his youth; nevertheless, Jesus still desired and required more of him. Jesus instructed the rich young ruler, "Go and sell all your possessions and give the money to the poor.... Then come, follow me" (Matt. 19:21 NLT). This passage reveals that knowing the commandments, and even religiously following them, is not what ultimately secures eternal life. This is important because our faith can become a checklist of dos and don'ts. Faith can become reduced to an internal experience that lacks outward manifestations (remember, as James 2:17 says, faith without works is dead) and relational fruit. When this happens, we mistake legalism for the gospel and mis-interpret dutifulness for faithfulness.

Jesus did not tell the rich young ruler to destroy or merely separate himself from his possessions. Jesus instead instructed him to distribute his wealth among the poor. Through this instruction, Jesus challenged the rich young ruler to recon-sider his orientation toward, and relationship with, the least of these. Jesus commissioned the rich young ruler to see himself as connected to the poor, as bound to his marginalized neighbors in the divine economy of the inbreaking kingdom. Jesus called the rich young ruler to understand that there was a connection between the excess in his life and the lack in his neighbors' lives.

Jesus ultimately called the rich young ruler to understand that he—as is also the case with you and me—was blessed to be a blessing. Followers of Christ do not have the option of hoarding wealth when we see our neighbors in need. Nor can we use that with which God has entrusted us exclusively for our personal gain or the enrichment of our biological family. Furthermore, we cannot restrict the beneficiaries of our wealth to those within our ancestral bloodlines. As followers of Christ, we have a biblical, theological, and ethical responsibility to sacrificially share our wealth with the poor and leverage the privilege, access, and resources with which we have been entrusted to further the kingdom on earth as it is in heaven.

In asking the rich young ruler to envision and enact this new posture toward the poor, Jesus implored the young man to begin identifying with the poor in new and radical ways. Jesus summoned him to explore new and creative avenues to faithfully steward all with which he had been entrusted. Ultimately, Jesus was calling the rich young ruler to live as a citizen of heaven by transcending the social barriers and constructs that dictate human interactions—especially between the haves and the have-nots—in worldly empires. Jesus commissioned the rich young ruler to do this because the world knows that we are his followers when we love one another. This love is most profoundly expressed across lines of difference and in relation to the least of these.

The cost of Christ's words ultimately constituted this man's grief; he decided to cling to his money, possessions, and privilege rather than fostering authentic communion with the poor. He refused to follow Jesus, partially due to his wealth, but also because his identity was so rooted in his social status and power.

Following Jesus would have meant laying down his life as he knew it. It would have meant truly dying to himself so that Christ could rise to live in and through him. Following Jesus would have meant that the rich young ruler could no longer serve two masters: money and God. When Jesus asked him to "choose this day whom you will serve," he chose to serve mammon.

Consequently, the rich young ruler refused to identify with the poor and therefore forsook the opportunity to participate in socioeconomic justice and kingdom restoration. Rather than intentionally leveraging his wealth, possessions, and power for justice to further the kingdom and love his disenfranchised neighbors, he chose self-centeredness. In the end, the cost of discipleship was too high for him. He chose what he knew—the financial, social, and political perks of this world—over the unknown. He elected privilege and the pleasures of this world over kingdom treasures.

Jesus calls his followers to a countercultural, sacrificial, and cruciform life. Christianity is not about internal morality or rigorously keeping a list of commandments. It is about becoming more like Jesus. As we grow in Christlikeness, our lives will become more reflective of the love, mercy, and justice of Jesus.[1]

Faithfully following Jesus requires us to ask, is the gospel still good news when it costs me something? Moreover, is the gospel of Jesus Christ still good news when it costs me *everything*? The gospel is not merely a get-out-of-hell-free card; it is a divine invitation to participation, to serve as colaborers with Christ in restoring all things—which includes not only broken people, but systems, structures, and communities that have been perverted by sin—to God.

Coheirs with Christ

Jesus is love enfleshed. He epitomizes self-giving love and illuminates why we must leverage and sometimes abandon privilege to further the kingdom and love our neighbors. Love compelled Jesus to forsake the shalom of heaven to enter the broken reality of our world to save us. Jesus sacrificially took on flesh—marginalized flesh—to endure the effects of sin, and ultimately sin itself, on our behalf to make reconciliation with God, neighbor, and creation possible.

God's love inspired the incarnation. John 3:16–17 reads, "For God so loved the world that he gave his one and only Son, that whoever believes in him shall not perish but have eternal life. For God did not send his Son into the world to condemn the world, but to save the world through him." Jesus did not have to become human—while remaining fully God—but was compelled by love to do so. Love, therein, prohibited Jesus from apathetically watching creation be destroyed by its captivity to sin, death, and the powers and principalities. Jesus responded to sin, evil, and the suffering they produce by entering in, intervening on our behalf, and standing in solidarity with creation. As Jesus' hands and feet in the world today, we follow his response to sin, evil, and suffering as our model.

Only Jesus fully embodies the salvific love of God. This

love bestows on us undeserved grace that saves, redeems, and adopts us into God's family. The grace-filled love of God, uniquely manifested in Jesus, gives us a new identity, purpose, and mission. Through it, we become children of God, colaborers with Christ, and ambassadors of reconciliation. Romans 8:17 reads, "Now if we are children, then we are heirs—heirs of God and co-heirs with Christ, if indeed we share in his sufferings in order that we may also share in his glory." This passage raises the question, What does it mean to share in Christ's sufferings? Moreover, how is the sharing of sufferings connected to the love of God? Philippians 2 gives us a framework to begin answering these questions.

Taking on the Mindset of Christ

Paul wrote in Philippians 2:1–8,

> If then there is any encouragement in Christ, any consolation from love, any sharing in the Spirit, any compassion and sympathy, make my joy complete: be of the same mind, having the same love, being in full accord and of one mind. *Do nothing from selfish ambition or conceit, but in humility regard others as better than yourselves. Let each of you look not to your own interests, but to the interests of others.* Let the same mind be in you that was in Christ Jesus,
>
> > who, though he was in the form of God,
> > did not regard equality with God
> > as something to be exploited,
> > but emptied himself,

> taking the form of a slave,
> being born in human likeness.
> And being found in human form,
> he humbled himself
> and became obedient to the point of death—
> even death on a cross. (NRSV, emphasis mine)

Few passages articulate Jesus' ethic of sacrificial love as comprehensively as the Christ hymn (vv. 6–11). When we take on the mindset of Christ, we do nothing out of selfish ambition or conceit and refrain from exploiting our status and positions for selfish gain. We also, in humility, empty ourselves for the sake of the kingdom and our neighbors. This entails standing in solidarity with our neighbors when we have the option not to, placing the interests of others before our own, and prioritizing the peace and prosperity of our community above our individual success—knowing that Scripture assures us that when our communities prosper, we do as well. In taking this Christlike posture, we move toward a collectivist pursuit of freedom, flourishing, and shalom.

After forsaking the shalom of heaven to enter the brokenness of our world (incarnation), Jesus leveraged his privilege to further the kingdom and love his neighbors. Jesus emptied himself by choosing not to exploit his status as fully God and fully man to avoid discrimination, persecution, and suffering for inaugurating the kingdom amid an oppressive empire with other values. Jesus was persecuted for extending the prophetic tradition of speaking truth to power, slandered for being a doctor to the sick, and rebuked for affirming the humanity in social outcasts. Nevertheless, Jesus chose to humble himself by pursuing the interest of others, and he made this choice, knowing it would mean enduring humiliation, torture, and death (crucifixion) for the sake of others.

This Philippians 2 passage describes how we can share in the sufferings of Christ, functioning as colaborers advancing the kingdom by sacrificially loving others. Christians are a peculiar people who no longer live for ourselves but die to ourselves so that Christ can rise and live in and through us. This requires humbly emptying ourselves and forsaking opportunities that exclusively benefit us and our biological family to pursue matters that further the kingdom and benefit our neighbors. It results in functioning as an interconnected body, meaning that when one part of the body hurts, we all hurt. We show up, speak up, and stand up when we see injustice happening to others. We choose solidarity when we have the privilege of staying above the fray, keeping our hands clean, or dismissing oppression because it does not directly impact us.

The pattern of this world seduces us into becoming workaholics with advanced degrees, who climb the socioeconomic ladder to make a good life for ourselves so our families can live in comfort and our kids can go to the best schools—so they can enter the rat race and do even better than we did. Hard work, education, and stability are great things, but when we are not mindful, they become idols and deter us from the *missio Dei*. We are created to worship God and to make our Creator's name known and love shown throughout the world. Two of the most profound ways we do this are by embracing a baptismal vision of belonging and leveraging what we have been entrusted with to bear witness to who and whose we are.

The gospel calls us to care for more than just our biological families. Scripture declares that we are our brother's keeper, that we have a responsibility to care for the poor, the vulnerable, and the least of these. New life in Christ liberates us from the bondage of rugged individualism and calls us into a life of mutuality, hospitality, and sacrificial love. Life in Christ gives us a new identity and a new family; it transforms the "us" and "them" categories that sustain worldly empires by creating an interdependent people who no longer choose apathy in the face of oppression, injustice, and systemic sin.

Paul used Jesus' life to explicitly compare what we *are not* to do as followers of Christ against what we *are* to do—empowered by the Spirit who dwells within us (verses 3 and 4 illustrate this). New Testament scholar Michael J. Gorman writes, "The Spirit dwells in our midst, not just in our hearts. The Spirit of cruciformity is the Spirit of Christian community, and it is by means of cruciformity that the Spirit produces unity."[2] Paul understood this passage as the story of Jesus' love for the world and as an exemplary story for the church. As people who find our identity in the love that was first shown to us by our Lord and Savior, we are called to offer this same spirit of love to our neighbors.

Christ's faith and obedience are expressions of his love for God and neighbor. Faith and love are not bifurcated; they are inherently connected. Therefore our faith in and love for God must be tangibly expressed in proclamation and demonstration. Our obedience to God and love for neighbor are testaments to the Spirit's work in our lives. Gorman explains, "The cross and resurrection [should] both motivate and shape daily life. The appropriate life 'for' or 'toward' Christ is the cruciform life. Life 'for' Christ, however, is simultaneously life 'for' others . . . because the cross and resurrection were for others."[3]

The cross is the unified expression of the faith and love of Christ, which produces a pattern of faith expressing itself in love for the church to follow. Jesus' faith in God's sovereignty resulted in unconditional love for us. Faith expressed in love is therefore the posture we are called to take before God in relation to neighbor. When we live in this manner, we take on the mindset of Christ, sharing in his sufferings to participate in the restorative work of God.

The Temptation of Jesus

After being baptized at the start of his ministry, Jesus was led by the Spirit into the wilderness. There he fasted for forty days and was tempted by the devil. Church historian Justo González writes, "The temptation of Jesus is not just one more attempt by the devil to hinder or undo God's work; it is an integral part of the mission of Jesus, who is to confront and destroy the powers of evil." González continues, "Jesus has to confront the powers of evil and conquer them. Ultimately, he will do this in the cross and resurrection. But now that struggle begins with the story of the temptation in the wilderness." [4]

In Luke's account of the first temptation, the devil tried to seduce a hungry Jesus to turn stones into bread and eat it. In the second temptation, the devil took Jesus to a high place to show him all the majesty of the kingdoms of the world. He then offered Jesus all the authority and splendor of those kingdoms if Jesus would worship him. In the third temptation, the devil led Jesus to Jerusalem and had him stand on the highest point of the temple. There the devil quoted Scripture to Jesus, saying, "If you are the Son of God . . . throw yourself down from here.

For it is written: 'He will command his angels concerning you to guard you carefully; they will lift you up in their hands, so that you will not strike your foot against a stone'" (Luke 4:9–11).

Each temptation represents a parallel temptation the devil used to lead Adam and then Israel to sin, and each signifies a different spiritual obstacle Jesus had to overcome to be faithful to his mission and purpose. Theologically, there are clear parallels between Jesus' temptation in the wilderness and Adam's temptation in the garden. González writes, "Just as Adam was tempted, so must Jesus be tempted; but while Adam succumbed to temptation, Jesus will stand firm. In the first round of the conflict the devil won; but now the devil will be thoroughly defeated by the work of Jesus."[5]

In the first temptation, Jesus was led by the Spirit into the wilderness to be tempted, and his fast in the wilderness was thus also guided and informed by the Spirit. If Jesus chose to turn the stones into bread and eat it, he would have broken his fast and mirrored Adam's disobedience by eating when he should not have.

In resisting the devil, Jesus quoted Deuteronomy 8:3, saying, "Man shall not live on bread alone." This quote ties Jesus' temptation to Israel's temptation in the wilderness. While Moses was leading the Israelites to the promised land, they were bewildered and famished (just as Jesus was), which caused them to question the validity of Moses' leadership. In the wilderness, Israel was tempted by Satan to give up on God's plan and return to Egypt and bondage. This temptation was about trusting God in trying times and believing that God's plan was sufficient.

In the second temptation, the devil demonstrated that he had the power to offer Jesus all the strength and splendor inherent in worldly kingdoms. González explains that "as a consequence of sin the present world is ordered in satanic fashion. It is a world of injustice and oppression. Such oppression and injustice are not merely the result of the will of oppressors, or of exploitation by the powerful; they are the result of evil's dominance over all of creation as a result of sin. The devil has the power to grant kingdoms."[6] The irony of this temptation was that the devil was offering Jesus something that would, in time, be his as King of Kings and Lord of Lords.

In the garden the devil also tempted Adam and Eve, telling them that if they ate from the forbidden tree, they would "be like God, knowing good and evil" (Gen. 3:5). This offer proved too tempting for them. This temptation was about power and patience.

In the third temptation, the devil tried to plant seeds of doubt in Jesus' mind—as he effectively did with Adam and Eve. After Eve told the serpent that they were forbidden from eating from the tree in the middle of the garden, Satan questioned what she said, responding, "You will not certainly die" (Gen. 3:4). This seed of doubt concerning what she knew to be true proved to be enough to spark her curiosity and led her and Adam into disobedience.

Satan questioned Jesus in an attempt to lure him into disobedience. Satan tried to plant seeds of doubt in Jesus' mind about his identity as the Son of God. After Jesus' baptism, "heaven was opened and the Holy Spirit descended on him in bodily form like a dove. And a voice came from heaven: 'You are my Son, whom I love; with you I am well pleased'" (Luke 3:21–22). Yet the devil tried to make Jesus question his identity by saying, "if you are the Son of God," then prove it. Jesus, however, knew that doing so would cause him to be disobedient and sin. Jesus combated Satan's challenge by quoting Scripture back to him. The passage he quoted was once again from Deuteronomy, when Moses led Israel through the temptations of the devil in the wilderness to the promised land: "Do not put the LORD your God to the test" (Deut. 6:16). The third temptation was about identity and sufficiency.

Luke wanted readers to recognize Jesus as the second Adam, the firstborn of re-creation. Luke indicated this by using the title "son of God" for both Adam (Luke 3:38) and Jesus (4:3). As the second Adam, Jesus came to undo the curse the first Adam initiated in the fall, but to do this Jesus had to face the same nature of the temptations to which both the first Adam and Israel succumbed. In those three temptations, the devil tried his best to lead Jesus astray during one of his weakest moments. Jesus, however, remained faithful amid the temp-tations, and throughout his lifetime he resisted temptations and was faithful to his mission, liberating us from the curse of the first Adam; the shackles of sin and death; and the rulers, authorities, powers of darkness, and principalities of evil in the heavenly realms.

Justo González writes that Luke uses

a double typology, in which the theme of Adam in the garden parallels the theme of Israel in the wilderness. Significantly, while the entire passage reminds us of the temptation of Adam in the garden, the string of quotes from Deuteronomy with which Jesus responds reminds us of the temptation of Israel in the wilderness. Thus the entire story of the exodus and the wanderings in the wilderness becomes a typological axis, showing that from ancient times God was beginning to undo the evil that was done in the fall.[7]

The Spirit of the Lord

After being tempted by Satan in the desert, Jesus returned to Galilee in the power of the Spirit. He went to the synagogue in his hometown, Nazareth, on the Sabbath and unfurled the scroll to read his mission statement from Isaiah 61. Jesus proclaimed, "The Spirit of the Lord is on me, because he has anointed me to proclaim good news to the poor. He has sent me to proclaim freedom for the prisoners and recovery of sight for the blind, to set the oppressed free, to proclaim the year of the Lord's favor" (Luke 4:18–19).

Context is needed to understand the significance of Jesus choosing to read from the prophet Isaiah. New Testament scholar Esau McCaulley writes,

Isaiah realized that true worship of Yahweh had implications for how one treated their neighbor. According to Isaiah, Israel's oppression of the poor in his day betrayed a practical apostasy. For Isaiah, piety must bear fruit in justice. Jesus knew that inasmuch as his message of justice impinged on the lives of the powerful, he was liable to rejection and death. Jesus not only embraced this prophetic tradition, he declared himself the climax of it by claiming that the acceptable day of the Lord (Is 61:1–2) had arrived in him (Lk 4:14–21). . . . Jesus saw his ministry as a part of a tradition of Israel's prophets who told the truth about unfaithfulness to God that manifested itself in the oppression of the disinherited.[8]

Jesus' synagogue declaration flowed from this prophetic tradition. The good news the Spirit empowered Jesus to proclaim was not simply about spiritual captivity, as it has too often been interpreted. In the Greek the word *ptochos*—used for "poor" in this passage—is not referencing spiritual poverty. The word signifies an economic class identity, meaning to be "reduced to beggary, begging, asking [for] alms." It can also be defined as "destitute of wealth, influence, position, honour." [9]

Similarly, the word for "oppressed" here is not simply about being spiritually oppressed. The Greek word used for oppression in this passage is *thrauō*. This is the only time in Scripture this tense of the word is used. The root word (*thrauō*) is used three other times in Scripture (Ex. 15:6; Num. 24:17; and Isa. 58:6), and it means "to break, break in pieces, shatter, smite through." [10] In Isaiah the word describes God's liberating action on behalf of the poor and oppressed. In Numbers and Exodus, the word describes God's physical intervention on behalf of Israel against their enemies. The Spirit of the Lord thus was upon Jesus to deal with sin, the oppression it causes, and the forces seeking to prohibit the people of God from fulfilling our created purpose.

The "year of the Lord's favor" is a reference to the Year of Jubilee, defined in Leviticus 25:8–55. Jubilee had radical economic and ethical implications for society. Jubilee was a time when stolen and seized land was returned to its original inhabitants, prisoners of debt and war were returned to their families, and the land was to be left untended to revitalize itself—with no attempt being made to store up the products of the land. [11] Jesus concluded his mission statement by declaring that he was the fulfillment of this text.

As theologian Drew Hart explains, "Jesus is not involved in a revolution in the traditional sense, but has inaugurated the reign of God, a new social order on earth, which is revolutionary and threatens the foundations of the old order." This new order is the upside-down kingdom. And the Gospels, Hart explains, reveal "how ethnic outsiders and Samaritans, vulnerable women, lepers, and the poor hungry masses are prioritized in Jesus' new order manifesting on earth." [12]

Jesus and the Disenfranchised

In his iconic text *Jesus and the Disinherited*, Howard Thurman wrote,

> Many and varied are the interpretations dealing with the teachings and the life of Jesus of Nazareth. But few of these interpretations deal with what the teachings and the life of Jesus have to say to those who stand, at a moment in human history, with their backs against the wall.
>
> To those who need profound succor and strength to enable them to live in the present with dignity and creativity, Christianity often has been sterile and of little avail. The conventional Christian word is muffled, confused, and too vague. Too often the price exacted by society for security and respectability is that the Christian movement in its formal expression must be on the side of the strong against the weak. This is a matter of tremendous significance, for it reveals to what extent a religion that was born of a people acquainted with persecution and suffering has become the cornerstone of a civilization and of nations whose

very position in modern life has too often been secured by a ruthless use of power applied to weak and defenseless peoples.[13]

Jesus could have come into the world as anyone from anywhere, but he chose to come as a helpless babe, born to impoverished parents in the ghetto of Galilee, Nazareth. Jesus had a death sentence placed on him by the most powerful man in the land at birth. He was forced to flee political persecution, migrating to a foreign land with his family for what would equate to asylum today and was later falsely arrested, tried, and crucified. Jesus knows what it is like to endure injustice, oppression, and systemic sin.

Jesus also concurrently epitomized privilege. Being fully God and fully man, Jesus had the opportunity and power to opt out of any suffering or persecution he desired. Nevertheless, he chose solidarity with humanity and, most explicitly, with the least of these. The most profound articulation of this is Matthew 25:31–46 (NRSV), where Jesus said, "Truly I tell you, just as you did it to one of the least of these who are members of my family, you did it to me" (v. 40). Jesus does not just randomly mention the hungry (Luke 4:2; 24:41), thirsty (John 19:28), stranger (Matt. 2:13–15), naked (Matt. 27:28; Luke 10:30), sick (Matt. 8:17), and prisoner (Matt. 27:17; Mark 15:9; Luke 23:18–19; John 18:12). Jesus was speaking from experience; he embodied each of these forms of marginality and, in doing so, prophetically stands in solidarity with those who have experienced marginality throughout the course of time.

However, Matthew 25:31–46 is not just about who Jesus was; it is about who the people of God are called to be. Christians are commissioned to be people who follow Jesus' example of going through, rather than around, Samaria. We follow Jesus into the slums, barrios, and favelas that the world and our well-intentioned parents tell us to avoid at all costs. We cross the tracks and dividing lines of society to go into conflictual territory; to intentionally breach socialized lines of clean and unclean, us and them, citizen and undocumented, free and prisoner; to bear witness to the inbreaking reign of God. We go to defamed places and spaces as colaborers, joining Jesus in the restorative work God is already up to—not only to bring the gospel, because it is usually already there.

We go to Samaria, embodying the gospel, to proclaim good news in word and deed. We go to bear witness to the power of the resurrection in hostile territory where death, oppression, and injustice have reigned too long. We go to express our faith in love to neighbors who need to see Christianity lived out and not just talked about. We go to recalibrate our vision, to learn to see our disinherited sisters and brothers as family, as people we are inherently connected to, and as equitable image bearers. We go to commune with our disenfranchised neighbors to learn from them because they have vitally important things to teach us, and to begin reimagining life together on earth as it is in heaven. Our presence in stigmatized spaces—when we take this posture—demonstrates that God still hears and responds to the anguished cries that arise from those who suffer. We therefore go to and through Samaria to show God's love, to learn how to effectively advocate for our forsaken neighbors, and to hold systems and structures accountable.

Bryan Stevenson describes how this upside-down kingdom logic concretely looks in the world. He says, "Many of us have been taught that if there's a bad part of town, you don't put your business there. But I am persuaded that we need to do the opposite. We need to engage and invest and position ourselves in the places where there is despair."[14] When we do so, we take on the mindset of Christ and follow our Lord and Savior's example, leveraging privilege to proclaim good news.

The gospel, Justo González writes, "is not good news for those who thrive on injustice, whose power is oppressive and unjust. For them, the good news is first of all the possibility—and the need—of what may well be a costly repentance."[15] Let us now turn in the next chapter to Zacchaeus, another person Jesus calls to a costly repentance, and unpack what bearing fruit in keeping with repentance entails.

Reflection Questions

1. Given that John 13:35 says, "By this everyone will know that you are my disciples, if you love one another," what keeps us from choosing to love one another?

2. First John 3:16 reads, "This is how we know what love is: Jesus Christ laid down his life for us. And we ought to lay down our lives for our brothers and sisters." How is God calling you to lay down your life for your brothers and sisters?

3. Our response to neighbors in need communicates something to the world. What does your response communicate?

4. How could taking on the mindset of Christ change the tenor of ecclesial conversations about movements for needed social change?

5. How do the Greek definitions of the words *poor* and
   oppressed shift how you understand Luke 4:18–19?

6. How is Matthew 25:31–46 prescriptive for who the
   church is called to be?

CHAPTER 7

ZACCHAEUS

Leveraging Privilege to Foster
Social Transformation

Economic justice is a consistent theme throughout Scripture, but too few congregations prioritize it. Often, discipleship has little to nothing to do with economic justice. We are taught to be compassionate and charitable, but do our churches, Bible colleges, and seminaries teach us to pursue economic justice? Does our lack of formation regarding economic justice inhibit us from developing an intelligible economic analysis that empowers us to make connections between wealth accumulation, oppression, and systemic sin? As we seek the peace and prosperity of our communities, laboring to cultivate just environments where all—not just some—of God's children can flourish, do we need a more robust biblical framework regarding economic justice?

Scripture tells us that "the love of money is a root of all kinds of evil" (1 Tim. 6:10). As we strive to resist and uproot evil, we must begin considering how our fiscal socialization implicitly impedes our ability to trace and expose the evil the love of money induces. Making money a taboo topic or something we are not taught to think theologically about inhibits us from thinking critically about income, examining how the rich acquire wealth, and showing how influential leaders and corporations have built lucrative legacies off oppression. Take slavery for instance; ten of the first twelve US presidents were slave owners, and eight owned slaves while serving as president. Eighteen of the first thirty-one US Supreme Court justices were slave owners.[1] Wall Street—the epicenter of capitalism in the US, if not the world—got its name from the slave trade, functioning as New York's primary slave market for more than fifty years, and the prosperity of many of the largest banking and insurance institutions is rooted in the violence, death, and destruction of the slave trade.[2]

In 2005 JPMorgan Chase, the largest bank in the US, acknowledged that between 1831 and 1865, two of its predecessor banks accepted approximately 13,000 slaves as collateral for loans, which empowered chattel slavery to expand in unprecedented ways. They ended up owning approximately 1,250 slaves as a result of defaulted loans. Similarly, New York Life, one of the nation's largest life insurance companies, held a third of its insurance policies on slaves by 1847, which ensured that slave owners would profit even when they abused and exploited enslaved people to the point of death.[3] Additionally, insurance companies played another invaluable role in the triangular slave trade: they allowed those stealing and trafficking Africans to take out insurance policies on the people they stole. This was imperative to the fiscal success of the triangular trade because at least two million Africans—15 percent of those trafficked from Africa—died during the infamous Middle Passage, and insurance companies made sure that even if a Black life ended, white profit remained intact. New York Life is now a US Fortune 100 company.[4]

Antebellum historians Sven Beckert and Seth Rockman, authors of *Slavery's Capitalism*, explain that "by virtue of our nation's history, American slavery is necessarily imprinted on the DNA of American capitalism."[5] The slave trade was not just lucrative for a privileged few; enslaved people in many ways were the capital from which US capitalism evolved. Scholar Matthew Desmond's research underscores this point. He found that "at the high of slavery, the combined value of all enslaved people was more than that of all railroads and all the factories of the nation combined."[6] And David Blight, a professor of American history at Yale University, found that by 1860, on the cusp of the Civil War, "there were more millionaires [all slaveholders] living in the lower Mississippi Valley than anywhere else in the United States. In the same year, the nearly 4 million American slaves were worth some $3.5 billion, making them the largest single financial asset in the entire US economy, worth more than all manufacturing and railroads combined."[7] The $3.5 billion that enslaved people were "worth" in 1860 would equate to more than $109 billion today, and this figure does not even factor in the commerce enslaved people produced, which undergirded the US economy not just in the South but in the North as well.

Tax Collecting: Money, Exploitation, and Systemic Sin

Our fiscal socialization also informs our interpretation of Scripture. While the Bible repeatedly acknowledges how the powerful exploit the poor using weighted scales and dishonest measurements, few Christian resources explain the depth and breadth of economic exploitation in Scripture. This is true despite prophets like Amos and Micah condemning Israel for their covenantal unfaithfulness when they enact usury and exploitation to rob the least of these. Amos proclaimed that the exploitation got so bad that Israel would "sell the innocent for silver, and the needy for a pair of sandals. They trample on the heads of the poor as on the dust of the ground and deny justice to the oppressed" (Amos 2:6–7). And God spoke through Micah, saying to Israel, "Am I still to forget your ill-gotten treasures, you wicked house, and the short ephah, which is accursed? Shall I acquit someone with dishonest scales, with a bag of false weights? Your rich people are violent; your inhabitants are liars and their tongues speak deceitfully" (Mic. 6:10–12). Given the frequency, intensity, and systemic nature of economic oppression in Scripture, why is the topic so scarcely addressed in discipleship resources, books, and curriculum? The insufficient attention given to economic exploitation impoverishes our reading of Scripture and prohibits us from understanding it as a foundational pillar of empire—then and now.

Biblical scholar Elsa Tamez—one of the few scholars who authentically addresses economic exploitation in Scripture—writes, "When injustice manifests itself in every aspect of a nation's life, we necessarily infer that the structures of violence are being condoned by the authorities or by influential persons such as rulers, prophets, priests, and the wealthy."[8] Her analysis is rooted in passages like Ecclesiastes 5:8–10, which elucidate that economic exploitation is a systemic endeavor. It reads,

If you see the poor oppressed in a district, and justice and rights denied, do not be surprised at such things; for one official is eyed by a higher one, and over them both are others higher still. The increase from the land is taken by all; the king himself profits from the fields.

Whoever loves money never has enough; whoever loves wealth is never satisfied with their income.

Scripture repeatedly condemns economic exploitation as systemic sin and denounces leaders who condone and collude with it. The primary group Scripture indicts for economic exploitation—outside of unethical kings and merchants—is tax collectors. Tax collection is stigmatized as one of the most unethical jobs in Scripture. Canonically, tax collectors are always tied to the most defamed groups, and this is because the vocation was rooted in abuse, coercion, and corruption. While Scripture alludes to the unethical nature of tax collectors, a deeper exploration into the mafia-like tactics employed while abstracting money will yield a greater understanding of why tax collectors were so notorious.

Theologian Pheme Perkins writes, "Early Christian thinking about taxation was shaped by an environment in which taxes were oppressive and rapaciously administered."[9] The Romans exacted water, city, food, road, house, temple, and frontier taxes from Palestinians. Historian Moses Finley explains, "The burden of taxation in the Roman providences fell unequally on different groups. It was heaviest on those who actually worked the land, the peasants and the tenant farmers."[10] This was uncommon practice in ancient times, particularly in this region, and it therefore stands as one of the reasons the Roman

Empire is so infamous. Finley expounds, writing, "While the Greek system had made the wealthy bear most of the cost of government, the Roman expansion shifted the tax burden to the subject peoples of the providences. Consequently, wealthy Romans did not bear the cost of government. It was passed down to the poorest members of society largely in land taxes."[11]

Although Roman taxes fiscally pressed the least of these, the straw that broke the camel's back was the economic exploitation enacted by corrupt Roman officials. These representatives, Moses Finley explains, accumulated much of their wealth through "the substantial amount [of taxation] that never reached the treasury but was diverted by a horde of tax-collectors and officials, partly as legal perquisites, partly as illegal exactions."[12] Theologian Adolf Hausrath asserts that the Roman tax system emboldened systemic sin by empowering immoral tax collectors to repress trade, with immunity, "to an unheard-of extent."[13] Describing the corrupt enterprise, Hausrath writes, "It was a favorite device of the tax-gatherers moreover, to advance money to those unable to pay, thus converting the tax into a private debt, upon which an usurious interest was exacted."[14]

New Testament and Greek professor Merrill Tenney wrote that tax collectors "were noted for their impositions, rapine and extortion, to which they were tempted to oppress the people with illegal taxes that they might more quickly enrich themselves."[15] Church historian Alan Campbell elucidates this by explaining how tax collectors enforced frontier taxes "at every stopping place some tax was levied. The result was that sometimes the price of a good exceeded 100 times its original cost."[16]

Moreover, historian Naphtali Lewis explains that tax

collectors also used imperial muscle to line their pockets. He writes, "The rapacity of tax-collectors, their use of soldiers to threaten and beat the populace, and the attempts to avoid such treatment by payment of bribes are all documented in inscriptions and court complaints."[17] Ultimately, Tenney concludes, "The Romans adopted the very cruel but efficient method of 'farming out the taxes' each officer extorting more than his share from those under him, and thus adding to the Jewish hatred of the publicans [another word used for tax collectors]."[18] This history contextualizes Luke 3:12–15, where John the Baptist rebuked tax collectors and soldiers—which, on the surface, seems like an odd pairing—for their corruption, extortion, and greed. Biblical scholar Lewis Muirhead explains, "The phrase 'publicans and sinners' (Luke XV 1; cp. Matt. XXI 31) is fair evidence not only of the extreme unpopularity of the customsmen as a class, but also of the fact that the associations of their office were such as to make honesty extremely difficult, though not impossible (Matt. XXI; cp. Luke III 12f.), to those who held it."[19]

Zacchaeus: The Chief Tax Collector

Rome had common and chief tax collectors. Chief tax collectors, like drug lords, extracted profit from the common tax collectors they supervised, who existed on a lower rung of the systemic food chain of oppression. Comparable to white-collar criminals today, chief tax collectors' fiscal flourishing was rooted in systemic sin. They profited from a depraved system that ensured the rich would get richer by oppressing the public and extorting the poor.

Jews therefore despised tax collectors. It was through tax collectors that they were subject to the Roman emperor. The paying of taxes was viewed as a recognition of the emperor's sovereignty. Biblical scholar Joseph Fitzmyer explains that "Jews who engaged in collecting tariffs, tolls, imposts, and customs for the Romans were under the double stigma of having bid for the office and of serving the occupying power."[20] Zacchaeus, as described in Luke 19:1–10, was such a stigmatized Jew.

Zacchaeus was conscripted by the Roman government to collect taxes from his fellow Jews in Jericho. As a chief tax collector, he engaged in criminal activity and became "very wealthy" because of it. Biblical scholar Justo González writes, "That Zacchaeus was rich implies that he was not just one of many tax collectors, but an important one. A sinner among sinners!"[21] Zacchaeus not only extorted his own people, but he also mercilessly preyed on the poor and vulnerable, charging them more than what they owed Rome to line his pockets.

Consequently, Zacchaeus's community despised him and saw him as a traitor. He was cut off from the covenant community, and we see the effects of this when Jesus came to town. While Sunday school taught us that Zacchaeus could not see Jesus because he was a wee little man, his vertical limitation was not the only reason he was unable to see Jesus. Zacchaeus was also unable to see Jesus because his peers were repulsed by him and saw him as their enemy. They therefore refused to assist, touch, or make room for him. Zacchaeus, because of his economic exploitation, found himself physically and socially isolated from both Jesus and his community.

Campbell explains, "Jews had such utter contempt for the publicans that money known to have come from them was not accepted at the synagogue or temple. It is apparent that few publicans would have had a chance to hear Christ's synagogue discourses. They would probably not have been admitted even if they had sought entrance."[22]

Zacchaeus, consequently, took drastic measures; he ran ahead of the crowd and climbed a sycamore tree to encounter Jesus. Jesus saw him and said, "Zacchaeus, come down immediately" (Luke 19:5). By calling Zacchaeus by name, Jesus signified that he knew Zacchaeus, his vocation, and everything it entailed. Jesus then breached the purity rituals and kinship norms of ancient Near Eastern society when he said, "I must stay at your house today," because Jesus would have become culturally unclean and disreputable by communing with an unethical renegade like Zacchaeus.

Jesus' interaction with Zacchaeus is framed by a previous interaction where Jesus was criticized for interacting and eating with another tax collector. In Luke 5 Jesus saw Levi, also a tax collector, and said to him, "Follow me." Luke 5:28 says, "Levi got up, left everything and followed him." Levi welcomed Jesus, his disciples, and a number of his tax collector friends into his house, and as they ate together, the Pharisees and the teachers of the law began criticizing Jesus, asking his disciples, "Why do you eat and drink with tax collectors and sinners?" Jesus answered, "It is not the healthy who need a doctor, but the sick. I have not come to call the righteous, but sinners to repentance" (vv. 30–32).

Call and Response

When Jesus went to Zacchaeus's home, he did not go just to engage in table fellowship—he went to heal the sick and to call Zacchaeus to repentance. In doing so, Jesus was bearing witness to the good news of the gospel, that even people like Zacchaeus who are steeped in oppression are not beyond redemption, nor are they destined to be forever defined by their past. Jesus gives anyone who comes into a revelation of their sinfulness—regardless of what they have done—an opportunity to contritely confess their sins, genuinely lament the harm they have caused, and soberly repent by turning away from their sins in order to return to God and reconcile with their neighbor.

The transformative power of the gospel frees us from having to live in shame or condemnation regarding our sins, and it also compels us to break toxic cycles of generational sin within our families (as Pharaoh's daughter shows). We all are offered unmerited grace from God. And we are all given the opportunity to make amends for our transgressions and the sins of our ancestors that we continue to benefit from, even if only passively. Empowered by the Spirit, all prodigal children—like me, you, and Zacchaeus—have an opportunity to bear witness to repentance by keeping with it in a manner that produces kingdom fruit.

Jesus called Zacchaeus to repent, and he responded by standing up and proclaiming, "Look, Lord! Here and now I give half of my possessions to the poor, and if I have cheated anybody out of anything, I will pay back four times the amount" (Luke 19:8). This proclamation demonstrated that Zacchaeus knew he exploited the poor, and he also understood that merely saying, "I'm sorry, Lord. I'm a sinner; please forgive me," while retaining the booty his sins commandeered, would have been insufficient. Zacchaeus understood that repentance required more than words. His repentant heart inspired him not only to give half of his possessions to the poor but also to calculate the cumulative effect his oppression had on families and the community and then commit himself to paying reparations accordingly.

Zacchaeus understood that his sins had created communal trauma and constructed a perpetual underclass. He knew that his economic exploitation harmed more individuals than the people he directly extorted. Zacchaeus acknowledged that the depraved system of tax collection generated oppressive patterns of debt, poverty, and abuse that had to be atoned for. When we are spiritually mature enough to soberly assess our sins and the collective impact they have had on our neighbors, the Spirit leads us to discern what true reconciliation requires.

For Zacchaeus, repentance and reconciliation required reparations. Zacchaeus paid a steep price to atone for the social impact of the systemic sin he supervised and engaged in. As a fruit of his repentance, Zacchaeus committed to doing his part to end the generational cycles of poverty and trauma his sins created and exacerbated, and he did so by enacting economic transformation within the community he robbed.

It was only after Zacchaeus committed to bearing fruit in keeping with repentance that Jesus declared, "Today salvation has come to this house." The salvation Jesus enacted in Zacchaeus's life was not purely personal. Salvation was not solely about Zacchaeus establishing a personal relationship with Jesus or about God restoring Zacchaeus's sense of peace and self-worth. Instead, through Zacchaeus's response to Jesus' call to repentance, we see that salvation requires repentance and repentance necessitates providing reparations to those harmed by our sins. As Jesus chose to bind himself to Zacchaeus in relationship, Zacchaeus had to reconcile himself to God and neighbor by choosing to bind himself to those he stole from by offering restitution for his sins.

Biblical scholar Elsa Tamez writes,

> In the New Testament there are very few instances in which the term *metanoia* means simply remorse. In the majority of the texts the meaning of *metanoia* is a radical change of outlook (accompanied, of course, by concrete actions). In its religious and ethical meaning the term is in the line of the Old Testament and Jewish concept of conversion. At the same time, however, the word in its New Testament usage conveys some ideas not found in the Old Testament. One of these is the pressing need of conversion to the kingdom of God, which is already at hand: "The time is fulfilled, and the Kingdom of God is at hand; repent, and believe in the gospel" (Mark 1:15).[23]

Jesus affirmed Zacchaeus's repentance by declaring that he was "a son of Abraham." Biblical scholar Dennis Hamm writes, "Zacchaeus shows himself to be a true son of Abraham in just the sort of conversion John the Baptist calls for in Luke 3:10–14. In his conversion he shows himself to be, like Abraham, one who shows his righteousness in deeds of hospitality."[24] As a son of Abraham, Zacchaeus was no longer defined by the oppression he enacted; he was now known as one who made reparations for his sins. He was no longer shunned by his peers, destined to exist in isolation, but was invited to become an active participant in covenant community. He was no longer an active participant in, or an unethical beneficiary of, an unjust system.

He was now one who was sacramentally bound to the poor. Jesus transformed a person who oppressively violated community into an advocate of justice and an indispensable member of God's family. This is what the gospel has the power to do when we engage in biblically based repentance.

To produce fruit in keeping with repentance, Zacchaeus had to soberly examine his rich legacy of economic exploitation, explore his ledger to identify everyone he robbed, expand this list to include not only those he robbed but also those affected by his sins, and then confess the specificity of his sins. After lamenting the social injustice and communal oppression his sins caused, he went out and faced his victims, acknowledging every person harmed by his economic exploitation. Zacchaeus therefore became a beautiful model of Christian repentance.

After encountering Jesus, Zacchaeus knew that he must turn away from sin and return to God. He understood that oral confession alone was inadequate. Zacchaeus did not try to absolve himself of his sins by saying, "I was just doing my job," or "There is no way I could know all of the people impacted by my sins beyond the people I directly defrauded." He was spiritually mature enough to realize that repentance is inconvenient and takes work.

While the entire system is guilty, as we work to transform broken systems, we also need eyes to see the people of God within these systems who need to be called to repentance. As the people of God who are integrated within broken systems and structures awaken to their sinful complicity and follow Zacchaeus's model, we establish kingdom pressure points that help us topple oppressive systems that counteract the will of God.

Tax collectors are repeatedly referenced as sinners (Matt. 5:46–47; cf. Luke 6:32–34) and called to repentance by Jesus (Matt. 9:12–13; Mark 2:17; Luke 5:31–32). In fact, Justo González points out that the "last person who repents and rejoices at Jesus' call is a rich tax collector."[25] Zacchaeus is the last of Luke's examples of the lost being found. Jesus also called Levi (also known as Matthew) to walk away from his profession as a tax collector to become one of his twelve disciples. Jesus' consistency in calling tax collectors to repentance is a clear reminder that we cannot serve two masters, and that irrespective of the harm one has caused, none one is beyond redemption.

Radical Transformation Still Happens

Claiborne Ellis, also known as C. P. Ellis, was the Exalted Grand Cyclops of the Ku Klux Klan in Durham, North Carolina. In 1971 he was invited to cochair a ten-day charette (a meeting of communal stakeholders who work to resolve conflicts and map solutions) with Ann Atwater—a local Black civil rights activist—in response to escalating racial tensions in Durham after a court-ordered mandate to integrate the city's public schools. The charette illuminated the power of proximity. Ellis's view of Black people evolved as he formed new relationships with Black community members and saw firsthand the gross injustices segregation bred.

On the final day of the charette, Ellis took the microphone, pulled out his KKK membership card, and said before the crowd, "If schools are going to be better by me tearing this card up, I will do so."[26] Ellis then went back to the Klansmen and told them he could no longer be their leader. Ellis, reflecting on renouncing his leadership position in the Klan, said, "You know the Klan really done something for me, gave me some standing and made me feel better. But . . . you know this business about every time people talk about the Klan, they talk about hating Niggers or something like that. But I don't feel like that about Black folks now; it just ain't there."[27]

Ellis, who grew up poor, was particularly transformed by the courageous leadership of Atwater—whose parents were impoverished sharecroppers. Their relationship helped Ellis realize that Black inferiority was not the city's problem. As Ellis saw beyond the white supremacist rhetoric he was immersed in, he started to understand that poor people did not just have common problems and concerns, but they also had an opportunity to collectively mobilize and work together for the common good. Ellis joined Atwater as a community development advocate, working to address inequities in education, to establish a living wage for all employees, and to overcome racist policies that produced and exacerbated disparities through the city. Ellis and Atwater formed a deep and lasting friendship spanning forty-five years, until Atwater died in 2016.[28] Their relationship and story was popularized by the 2019 film *The Best of Enemies*.

You Cannot Crucify What You Cannot Name

Bryan Stevenson and the Equal Justice Initiative (EJI) are committed to pursuing truth and reconciliation and doing so in that order. EJI erected the National Memorial for Peace and Justice in Montgomery, Alabama, in 2018, the first memorial dedicated to the legacy of Black people terrorized by lynching in the United States. EJI staff traveled coast to coast to hundreds of lynching sites to diligently conduct archival and investigative research, collecting soil and interviewing families, historians, and civic leaders. (EJI collects soil from the sites of lynchings to dignify lynching victims who had their bodies desecrated and discarded.) EJI transformed its findings into an interactive memorial that demonstrates how racial terror lynchings ravaged the US, and exemplifies the depth and breadth of lament our nation should be engaging in because of these terror lynchings. The Memorial for Peace and Justice is intended to reshape the nation's cultural landscape and foster a more truthful and accurate historical narrative.

The Memorial for Peace and Justice features sculptures, art, and design that animate the horrid history of racial terror. At its epicenter stands a memorial square with eight hundred six-foot monuments to symbolize thousands of racial terror lynching victims, with each six-foot monument representing a different county and state where a lynching took place. Each monument documents the name(s) of lynching victims and the date(s) of their murder(s). EJI understands that we cannot crucify what we cannot, or will not, name. Therefore EJI strategically replicated each monument, installing one within the memorial and placing the replica just outside of the memorial, in hopes that each county would come, see, and claim its monument. After a county claimed its replica monument, EJI would help the community discern where it should erect the monument to foster a communal dialogue whereby the community could truthfully reckon with its history to cultivate a brighter future. EJI hopes the National Memorial inspires communities nationwide to enter an era of truth-telling about racial injustice, their own local histories, and how we can begin to truly pursue beloved community and life together.

In an interview with broadcaster and founder of The On Being Project Krista Tippett, Bryan Stevenson said,

> We have a project that we're starting—it's called the Truth and Justice Project. And we're actually gonna be working with institutions, asking them to focus on their institution—to step back, put aside all the global stuff. And it began, really, in 2018 when we were opening the memorial. The local newspaper, the *Montgomery Advertiser*, was kind of complaining a little bit. They said, oh, we know you're gonna talk to *The New York Times* and *The Washington Post* and all of these other— but you won't talk to us. [laughs] And I said, well, let's have a conversation about that.
>
> And we showed them their coverage, their media, their coverage of lynchings that took place in this area, early in the twentieth century. And you read it, and it breaks your heart. They were absolutely encouraging this violence. And I said, "If you ask me why don't I trust you, it's rooted in my knowledge of this history."
>
> And we started a dialogue, and the editor didn't know about any of that stuff, but when we confronted him, he says, "You know what? We have to apologize." I said, "I think that would be really powerful." And on the opening, they did this massive headline, massive front page, a whole edition dedicated to apologizing for their role in contributing to racial terror, lynchings, in this community. And it was really powerful. And I thought, well, after the *Montgomery Advertiser*

did this, lots of newspapers are going to do that. And the truth is, nobody else did it. And that's because that instinct to not tell the truth if you don't have to, to not confront these problems, is so powerful.

But this project that we're doing is a project that is going to encourage these institutions to do exactly what the *Advertiser* did in that setting. We have banks that denied mortgages and loans to Black veterans after World War II and created the wealth gap that we still see today. And I think they need to own that. We have institutions in this country that refused to provide coverage on insurance plans when Black people were forced off their lands as a result of racial violence. And I think we need to own that.[29]

While the *Montgomery Advertiser*'s courageous confession did not initiate the tidal wave of confession and repentance Stevenson was hoping for, *The Kansas City Star*—one of the most prestigious newspapers in the Midwest—did follow suit on December 20, 2020. It published a cover story titled "The Truth in Black and White: An Apology from *The Kansas City Star.*"

The article began with this confession:

Today we are telling the story of a powerful local business that has done wrong.

For 140 years, it has been one of the most influential forces in shaping Kansas City and the region. And yet for much of its early history—through sins of both commission and omission—it disenfranchised, ignored and scorned generations of Black Kansas Citians. It reinforced Jim Crow laws and redlining. Decade after early decade it robbed an entire community of opportunity, dignity, justice and recognition.

That business is *The Kansas City Star*.

Before I say more, I feel it to be my moral obligation to express what is in the hearts and minds of the leadership and staff of an organization that is nearly as old as the city it loves and covers:

We are sorry.

The Kansas City Star prides itself on holding power to account. Today we hold up the mirror to ourselves to see the historic role we have played, through both action and inaction, in shaping and misshaping Kansas City's landscape.

It is time that we own our history.

It is well past time for an apology, acknowledging, as we do so, that the sins of our past still reverberate today.[30]

In what the paper called "a full-blown examination" of its coverage of race and the Black community dating to its founding in 1880, the paper examined archives of *The Star* and what was once its sister paper, *The Kansas City Times*. This research was conducted because *The Star* believes that owning its past can help it move forward in a more faithful manner. In a six-part series, *The Star* acknowledged its power and influence, how it shaped attitudes in and around the city regarding racism, injustice, and systemic sin.

The paper admitted,

Reporters felt regret that the papers' historic coverage not only did a disservice to Black Kansas Citians, but also to white readers deprived of the opportunity to understand the true richness Black citizens brought to Kansas City. Like most metro newspapers of the early to mid-twentieth century, *The Star* was a white newspaper produced by white reporters and editors for white readers and advertisers. Having *The Star* or *Times* thrown in your driveway was a family tradition, passed down to sons and daughters.[31]

The paper also acknowledged,

In the pages of *The Star*, when Black people were written about, they were cast primarily as the perpetrators or victims of crime, advancing a toxic narrative. Other violence, meantime, was tuned out. *The Star* and *The Times* wrote about military action in Europe but not about Black families whose homes were being bombed just down the street. Even the Black cultural icons that Kansas City would one day claim with pride were largely overlooked. Native son Charlie "Bird" Parker didn't get a significant headline in *The Star* until he died, and even then, his name was misspelled and his age was wrong.[32]

The paper even confessed how it continued to miss the mark after diversifying in the 1960s, hiring Black reporters.

In 1968, five Black men and one Black teenager were killed over three days of rioting in Kansas City at the time the Rev. Martin Luther King Jr. was to be buried, having been assassinated by a white man's bullet only days prior. At least four and perhaps all were shot by police. A mayor's commission determined that most were "innocent victims," and yet there was no follow-up newspaper probe as there would be today, no independent investigation, no calls for the officers to be charged, or for the police chief to resign.[33]

After *The Star* articulated its growing commitment to racial justice, it encouraged "other Kansas City businesses to come forward and own their history as well, tell their stories, get the poison out—for the sake of the community and their employees."[34] Truth-telling, confession, and lament engender repentance, and keeping with repentance is what leads to kingdom transformation and authentic reconciliation.

Institutional Reparations Are Possible

The US has done everything in its power to avoid meaningful conversations about reparations that would translate into tangible, restorative action in response to stolen Indigenous land and chattel slavery. These sins, if acknowledged, are usually dismissed by skeptics as too ancient to be relevant today or to be responsibly addressed, and too immense to be adequately attended to. These objections have stifled constructive dialogue about reparations to the extent that many people, particularly Christians, have never been challenged to authentically consider if reparations are warranted and to imagine what this could entail.

However, times are changing, and the emerging generation is summoning our nation to consider reparations anew. Here are three examples of reparations given in different ways for egregious historical abuses of privilege.

Georgetown University

Instead of waiting for the school to act, Georgetown University students voted in 2019 to tax themselves to offer reparations to descendants of enslaved people. Their actions led to the school agreeing to commit to give $400,000 a year to benefit the descendants of the 272 enslaved people who were sold to help keep the college alive almost two centuries ago. The university will use the money to support community projects, such as health clinics and schools. The school only agreed to take these actions after its students exercised their voices. The school made their announcement concerning reparations six months after the students voted.[35]

The Treaty of Fort Laramie

The 1851 Treaty of Fort Laramie designated land near what is now downtown Denver to the Arapaho tribe. Four years after the treaty was signed, gold was discovered in the Rocky Mountains. The discovery of gold led to the Pikes Peak gold rush and inspired Colorado territorial officials to lobby federal authorities to alter the lines of what had been previously designated Indigenous land.

In 1861 the Fort Laramie treaty was broken, and Arapaho chiefs were coerced into ceding most of their land. Consequently, the Arapaho and other Indigenous people were forced into a small area in southeastern Colorado near the Arkansas River and a tributary called Sand Creek. On November 29, 1864, at the crack of dawn, the Sand Creek massacre transpired. A group of Cheyenne and Arapaho people, mainly women, children, and old men, were ambushed by seven hundred Colorado cavalry under the command of Colonel John Milton Chivington.

Chivington, who was a respected Methodist minister, told his officers the night before the raid, "Don't spare the children, the babies, because nits make lice."[36] Chivington, wanting to leave no stone unturned, later returned with his men to exterminate any wounded Indigenous people who survived the initial raid.

Fifteen years after the Sand Creek massacre, Bethany Danish Lutheran Church was founded on land that was included in the initial Treaty of Fort Laramie. When Bethany Church closed in 1973, the building became the property of the American Lutheran Church, which in 1988 transferred it to the Rocky Mountain Synod of the Evangelical Lutheran Church in America. Two years prior, in 1986, a group that would become formally known as the Four Winds American Indian Council had begun using the building as a sacred space and community center. George Tinker—an elder in the Four Winds community from the Osage Nation, professor emeritus at Iliff School of Theology in Denver, and an ordained Lutheran pastor—led the Four Winds community in reviving and embracing Indian spirituality. For twenty years Four Winds used the building to serve Denver's roughly forty thousand Indigenous people.

In 2010 the property's neighborhood began gentrifying, and the Rocky Mountain Synod considered selling the building and land. An interested buyer was willing to pay a million dollars for the property. But a concerned Lutheran pastor, Dena Williams, heard about the offer for the property and intervened. Williams feared that the Four Winds community would be displaced, so she contacted Tinker, whom she had developed a relationship with during her studies at Iliff. Over the next three years, the Four Winds Council met with Williams. During their meetings, the possibility emerged that the land could be given to the Four

Winds Council, but Williams learned that there were cultural obstacles that could prohibit this from happening.

Williams said, "Some Four Winds members were adamantly opposed to the entire concept of ownership of land. There was unwillingness to seek legal status as a nonprofit organization."[37] Nevertheless, as conversations continued, Rocky Mountain Synod bishop Jim Gonia began to develop a relationship with the Four Winds Council, and he said, "I think there was a ton that we, as the church, didn't know. We didn't know about the reality of Native American history in this country, about the continued marginalization of American Indian folk in our own community, and about their spiritual life, which is so important."[38]

Eventually, Four Winds was granted nonprofit status in late 2014. In early January 2015, the Four Winds Council and a Rocky Mountain Synod task force jointly drafted a letter requesting that the synod transfer the property to Four Winds. The synod council voted unanimously to transfer the deed.

In March a ceremony took place at Four Winds to mark the transfer, and in an interview about the ceremony, Williams said, "I spoke not of donating, but of returning sacred land to my American Indian brothers and sisters, as it never belonged to us in the first place."[39] Similarly, Bishop Gonia spoke at the ceremony, saying, "The white American thing would be to make a profit off this building, which was sitting in a critical spot in Denver and could have netted possibly a million dollars. But it wasn't the right thing to do. The right thing to do is to recognize that the ministry that had been taking place there for the last 20 years really represented the origins of that land to begin with."[40]

Jon Burge and the Midnight Crew

Vietnam veteran Jon Burge joined the Chicago police in 1970 and quickly moved up the ranks to commander. For nearly twenty years, from 1972 through 1991, Burge served as commander and oversaw what was known as a "midnight crew" that systematically tortured Black suspects.[41]

Stories of the violence committed under Burge—including beatings, electric shocks to the genitals and other body parts, suffocation with typewriter covers, mock executions, beatings, games of Russian roulette, and threats of being thrown out of windows—began to surface, and he was fired by 1993. In 2011 Burge was convicted on perjury charges for lying in civil lawsuits connected to torture.[42]

Forty-three years after Burge tortured the first known detainee, a resolution finally passed, providing compensation, restitution, and rehabilitation to survivors. This was a landmark reparations package; it was the first time survivors of racially motivated police torture had received reparations that they were entitled to under international law. Decades after being tortured by Burge and his crew, fifty-seven people—almost exclusively Black and from the south side of the city—received reparations totaling $5.5 million from the city of Chicago in 2016. Statutes of limitations on torture have prevented Burge and the detectives under his command from being prosecuted for torturing more than a hundred people.[43] The $5.5 million paid in these torture lawsuits was in addition to the more than $100 million that has been paid in court-ordered judgments, settlements of lawsuits, and legal fees over the years related to the Burge torture scandal.[44]

Corruption, abuse, and obstruction of justice weren't the

only injustices committed; several wrongly convicted Black people also spent years behind bars, like Alton Logan, who spent twenty-six years in prison for a murder he did not commit. Reparations do not right these wrongs, but as Zacchaeus's story shows, they are a tangible step toward reconciliation, restoration, and keeping with repentance.

What Can Everyday People Do?

Kaitlin Perez is a personal friend and former participant in Sankofa, the immersive discipleship experience I lead, which I mentioned in chapter 1. She beautifully exemplifies how to leverage privilege to further the kingdom and love neighbors in practical, everyday ways. I interviewed Kaitlin about her journey and asked her how she came to understand the subversive nature of the gospel. She said that she has come to realize that resources are like water—they need to flow through the people of God, particularly those of us with privilege, throughout the world.

Kaitlin explained that her journey began when she realized that as an upper-middle-class white woman, she was born into "unearned plenty." She said, "I did absolutely nothing to earn the wealth and privilege that has trickled down to me." While acknowledging and respecting the hard work and sacrifices her ancestors made to generate the resources at her disposal, she also recognizes that "my parents, grandparents, and great-grandparents were swimming with the tide and had systems and structures that aided their flourishing and wealth accumulation." Kaitlin then said, "But I did nothing to earn it." This is how the privilege of generational wealth works.

As Kaitlin learned more about our nation's unjust scales

and what Scripture says about justice, shalom, and stewardship, she realized there was more to wealth accumulation than what she had been taught in her youth. As her discipleship exposed the flaws in metanarratives like rugged individualism, being self-made, and pulling oneself up by the bootstraps, Kaitlin truly began to reckon with our nation's history of injustice and exclusion. She remembered feeling "convicted about how much I had financially when so many of my neighbors experienced financial hardship."

Kaitlin said, "Like most people, I resisted the truth about my privilege for a while, and once I accepted it, I had to work through white guilt. Initially, I just wanted to distance myself from the resources; and from a place of guilt, I felt an urge just to give it all away." As she matured in her faith, she said, "I began to shift from white saviorism into developing real relationships—particularly with Black women—that helped me understand that I was merely a vessel of God's grace, and that my material privilege could be strategically leveraged."

Kaitlin described going through a season of deep emptying, lament, and discipleship—which included participating in Sankofa—that helped her "focus on being obedient to God and accountable to my neighbors." She recalled it as a season "where I realized, while I possess these resources, they are not mine; they are God's. So I am just a conduit. I then began to move toward strategically leveraging the resources I have been entrusted with versus just abandoning them out of guilt."

Kaitlin described her revelation about abundance, explaining, "The world defines abundance as more, more, more, while the gospel defines abundance as having enough." God created enough for everyone's need but not enough for everyone's greed.

Her revelation took me back to the exodus, where God rained manna from heaven and instructed Israel to take only what they needed for the day. They were told that if they took more than what they needed, it would rot. Some greedy people tested God, and their food spoiled.

The Lord's Prayer has become a guiding principle for Kaitlin's life. She commonly meditates on the line "Give us this day our daily bread." She has wrestled with what it means to find contentment in "having enough for today." As a family of three, the Perezes have asked sober questions about what it means to have more than enough and how this excess is connected to their neighbors' lack of and need for daily bread.

Kaitlin has intentionally sought ways to leverage her resources and social capital to love her neighbors. The Holy Spirit led her to use her social network and financial resources to secure legal representation and post bond for someone who has since become a close friend. Kaitlin has invited her extended family to participate in economic and restorative justice by using their talents to sacrificially love their neighbors. She helped raise $20,000 for three Black businesses in February of 2020, which helped these institutions stay alive when COVID-19 hit a month later. The Perezes have moved from charity into strategically investing in business stimulation and wealth creation within disenfranchised BIPOC communities. Kaitlin has concluded, "If we didn't keep the flow going, we'd become a stopgap. And the blessings and resources were meant to flow through us and not just to us."

Kaitlin now has a new lens through which she sees the many ways her privilege manifests throughout everyday life. Ironically, a family funeral was one illustration of this. As she was making plans to travel to attend the funeral, her parents called and offered to cover all costs for the entire family. This generous offer brought to mind all the times she had heard friends struggling to make ends meet to attend to family emergencies. She realized in that moment that the money she would have spent to attend this funeral was now free to support their neighbors and friends who did not have the same privilege she did.

Kaitlin cited Luke 5 as a passage that keeps her humble and dependent on God. It reminds her that she is merely a willing vessel. God makes her love and support possible. She said, "In the passage, the fishermen try it on their own first, but when they obey Jesus and drop their nets where he instructs them to, they reap a harvest greater than they could have imagined. God instructs, and we obey. We are just willing vessels. All we're called to do is ask God, listen, and obey."

This is a beautiful model for demonstrating and proclaiming the good news of Jesus Christ. As we seek to produce fruit in keeping with repentance, Kaitlin's story helps us see that the fruit we produce begins with acknowledgment and confession, grows in our lament, and ripens in our obedience.

What Does Repentance Look Like for Me?

Might the Lord also be calling you to repentance, to walk away from your job because, as a beloved child of God, you cannot do it with integrity? Might God be calling you to abandon your esteemed position because it asks you to make concessions to your faith in order to move up the systemic food chain? Are there things your job requires of you that you need to confess and repent for, that make you complicit in systemic sin and oppression? May God be calling you to explore the roots of your familial inheritance? If you find that your inheritance or estate are rooted in sin and exploitation, what does it look like for you to heed John the Baptist's call to bear fruit in keeping with repentance? May the Lord be using Zacchaeus to show you that reparations are a part of what repentance and reconciliation entail for you?

If so, I want to invite you to follow the prompting of the Spirit! Freedom comes when we follow the Spirit into the wilderness and develop the faith needed to liberate ourselves from the imperial chains of exploitation. When we move from an individualist to a collectivist definition of freedom, we join the great cloud of witnesses upheld in this book, existing in the boundless and restorative love of God.

Reflection Questions

1. How does knowing more about the oppression that made tax collecting such a lucrative vocation change your understanding of this passage from Luke 19?
2. Repentance is often something we avoid, but why is repentance a gift?
3. The gospel declares that no one is beyond redemption. How does Zacchaeus bear witness to this?
4. Zacchaeus went from being a despised traitor to a critical contributor to communal flourishing. How does this passage illuminate the power of the gospel and repentance?
5. Why is it significant that Jesus did not declare, "Today salvation has come to this house" until after

Zacchaeus committed to bearing fruit in keeping with repentance?

6. The church typically talks about reconciliation without reparations, but reparations are a vital part of Zacchaeus's reconciliation story. How should this passage inform our reconciliation conversations?

CHAPTER 8

SCRIPTURE'S CALL
TO REPENTANCE

*We will have to repent in this generation not
merely for the hateful words and actions of the
bad people but for the appalling silence of the
good people. Human progress never rolls in on
wheels of inevitability; it comes through the
tireless efforts of men willing to be coworkers
with God, and without this hard work, time itself
becomes an ally of the forces of social stagnation.*
—Martin Luther King Jr.,
"Letter from a Birmingham Jail"[1]

Dr. King wrote his legendary "Letter from a Birmingham
Jail" in response to eight white clergymen who collab-
orated to compose and publish a letter in the local paper
vilifying his pastoral leadership and the campaign of militant,
nonviolent direct-action he was in Birmingham to help lead.

These clergy unified to halt justice and sustain white supremacy. They abused their power and platform to denounce protests as unwarranted and divisive, while calling Black residents "to withdraw support from these demonstrations."[2] These pastors used their influence to resist the freedom the Spirit was willing into existence. Lamentably, this was not the first or the last time clergy—particularly white clergymen—have mobilized around their self-interest rather than the gospel of Jesus Christ.

Tragically, King's words are as convicting, relevant, and true today as when he penned them in 1963. Too many clergy continue to use their platform and influence to suppress freedom instead of discipling their members to help usher in the kingdom on earth as it is in heaven. The lack of biblical discipleship in these congregations breeds idolatry. Consequently, too many people in our churches cling to a faith made in our image instead of God's. When we choose comfort and the status quo over Scripture's call to be ambassadors of reconciliation and colaborers with Christ, we sin. And Scripture is clear, when we sin, we must confess, lament, and repent.

This chapter examines why Dr. King's call to repentance is still so relevant. It lays bare the consequences of conforming to the patterns of this world and shows why the status quo is antithetical to the inbreaking kingdom of God. This chapter outlines what the Bible says about corporate and generational sin. It describes how remembrance, confession, lament, and repentance free us from sin's power. It concludes by explaining how seeking the kingdom first and pursuing shalom leads us to sacrificially love our neighbors and get into some good trouble.

Killing for Sport

One stop on Sankofa is the National Memorial for Peace and Justice—the first national memorial dedicated to the legacy of Black people who were lynched to reinforce white supremacy and constructed lines of racial purity (see chapter 7).

Black people were relentlessly terrorized by white vigilantes—with impunity—after the Emancipation Proclamation, as soon as the Reconstruction Era culminated. From 1865 to 1877, more than two thousand African Americans were lynched.[3] For eighty-seven consecutive years, from 1865 to 1952, at least one Black person was lynched every single year in the US.[4] Lynchings, however, did not stop in 1952; this was just the first year there was any sort of reprieve. The number of Black people lynched between 1880 and 1968 averages out to a Black person being lynched weekly for eighty-eight consecutive years.[5] Very conservative estimates conclude that at least sixty-five hundred Black people were murdered in this barbaric manner.[6] Between 1880 and 1890, the number of Black people who were lynched equates to a person every other day.[7]

Black people were lynched for trivial and usually falsified claims. These citizens were denied their civil right to due process and to be judged by a jury of their peers. BIPOC (Black, Indigenous, People of Color) citizens were categorically denied this right until the passage of the 1965 Voting Rights Act. Lynched Black bodies became so commonplace they became known as "strange fruit."

"Strange Fruit" was the title of a poem written in 1937 by Abel Meeropol, a Jewish teacher in the Bronx who saw a postcard of the lynching of two African American teenagers, Thomas

Shipp (eighteen) and Abram Smith (nineteen), in the town center of Marion, Indiana, before a crowd of ten thousand. The barbarity of this lynching haunted Meeropol to the point that he had to process it through crafting a poem of lamentation. Meeropol, who was also a composer, paired the poem's lyrics with music, and the resulting song was famously performed by Billie Holiday. In 1999 *Time* magazine named "Strange Fruit" the "song of the century," and the Library of Congress put the song in the National Recording Registry.

White lynch mobs were empowered by elected officials who embraced white supremacy. For example, James K. Vardaman, the governor of Mississippi, declared before his constituents in 1907, "If it is necessary, every Negro in the state will be lynched; it will be done to maintain white supremacy."[8] As much as we want to believe Vardaman was an anomaly, he was not. Cole Blease, the two-time governor and US senator from South Carolina, made a parallel proclamation, declaring that "lynching is a 'divine right of the Caucasian race to dispose of the offending Blackamoor without the benefit of jury.'"[9] Emboldened by elected officials who subscribed to white supremacist ideology and churches unwilling to denounce white supremacy as incongruent with Christianity, many saw lynchings—particularly spectacle lynchings—as a beloved national pastime.

Spectacle lynchings were akin to professional sporting events today. They were a carnival-like environment full of concession stands, vendors, photographers, and reporters, where thousands of eager fans gathered to participate in the mutilation, arson, and murder of Black bodies for entertainment. Twenty thousand people traveled to Owensboro, Kentucky, to participate in Rainey Bethea's lynching,[10] fifteen thousand gathered in Omaha, Nebraska, to participate in Will Brown's lynching,[11] and fifteen thousand convened in Waco, Texas, in front of the city hall to participate in the lynching of Jesse Washington, a cognitively impaired seventeen-year-old whom the mob stripped naked, repeatedly stabbed, brutally beat, and savagely mutilated before burning him alive.[12] The dismembered parts of Washington's body were sold as souvenirs, and the charred remains of his body were dragged from the back of a pickup truck, paraded through the Black community as a PSA to remind Black people of the deathly power of white supremacy.

Some may wish to scapegoat the South for the mortifying barbarism of spectacle lynchings, but many of the largest ones occurred in the Midwest and elsewhere. For instance, ten thousand gathered in Duluth, Minnesota, armed with bricks, rails, and heavy timbers. They broke into a jail with little resistance from law enforcement, abducted Elias Clayton, Isaac McGhie, and Elmer Jackson, and lynched them.[13] Five-thousand gathered in Springfield, Missouri, to lynch Horace Dunn and Fred Coker.[14]

Many of our nation's history books exclude this shameful piece of US history and others like it, including Chinese residents being forcefully expelled from more than forty cities by vigilante violence, the sexual abuse and ideology of white supremacy that hallmarked Indigenous boarding schools, and the economic exploitation and racism that gave rise to the United Farm Workers movement. Nevertheless, it is crucial that the church address spectacle lynchings. They occurred most often on Sunday afternoons after church, and they were well attended by white Christians. Speaking to this reality, Reinhold Niebuhr wrote, "If there was a drunken orgy somewhere I would bet ten to one a church member was not in it. . . . But if there was a lynching, I would bet ten to one a church member was in it."[15]

The Violence of 2020

Ahmaud Arbery was a twenty-five-year-old Black man who was murdered while jogging in his neighborhood near Brunswick, Georgia. He was preyed upon by armed white vigilantes carrying on the sinful American tradition of hunting Black bodies. A father, son, and their neighbor deputized themselves and killed Arbery in broad daylight on February 23, 2020. No arrests were made until May 5, and they were only made then because footage of the murder was leaked, sparking national outrage. If concerned citizens did not raise their moral voices collectively, these three men probably would not have been held accountable for murdering Arbery.[16]

Three weeks later, Breonna Taylor was killed in her home by an officer executing a no-knock warrant. The officer who killed Taylor "disobeyed rules and regulations" of the department, and the chief of police said Brett Hankison's "actions displayed an extreme indifference to the value of human life." The chief expounded, saying Hankison "wantonly and blindly fired ten (10) rounds" into Taylor's apartment on March 13, 2020.[17] Nevertheless, Hankison remained on the force until June 19 and was not charged for killing Taylor. If concerned citizens had not protested for more than one hundred consecutive days, calling for systemic and judicial accountability, Hankison would probably still be on the force, and even the slap on the wrist the involved officers received never would have happened.

On May 25, 2020, the world witnessed George Floyd unsuccessfully plead for his life as Derek Chauvin mercilessly knelt on his neck, using his body weight to constrict and ultimately terminate his breath. One would have hoped that Eric Garner, in 2014, would have been the last Black man to beg for his life in this manner, wailing, "I can't breathe," as an officer exerted deadly force. Lamentably he was not. While Chauvin was convicted of second-degree unintentional murder, third-degree murder, and second-degree manslaughter, his conviction probably would not have happened if not for Darnella Frazier's video and the global movement it inspired.

In response to this horrid string of violence, the lack of judicial accountability for taking Black lives, and the historic onslaught against Black life—particularly in the US, but also around the world in general—global protest ensued. Our nation was yet again engulfed in the ferocious flames of racial injustice.

Generational Sin and
Corporate Responsibility

Isabel Wilkerson, the first African American woman to win a Pulitzer Prize in journalism, offers a metaphor for generational sin and corporate responsibility in *Caste: The Origins of Our Discontents*:

> With an old house, the work is never done, and you don't expect it to be. America is an old house. We can never declare the work over. Wind, flood, drought, and human upheavals

batter a structure that is already fighting whatever flaws were left unattended in the original foundation. When you live in an old house, you may not want to go into the basement after a storm to see what the rains have wrought. Choose not to look, however, at your own peril. The owner of an old house knows that whatever you are ignoring will never go away. Whatever is lurking will fester whether you choose to look or not. Ignorance is no protection from the consequences of inaction. Whatever you are wishing away will gnaw at you until you gather the courage to face what you would rather not see.

We in the developed world are like homeowners who inhabited a house on a piece of land that is beautiful on the outside, but whose soil is unstable loam and rock, heaving and contracting over generations, cracks patched but the deeper ruptures waved away for decades, centuries even. Many people may rightly say, "I had nothing to do with how this all started. I have nothing to do with the sins of the past. My ancestors never attacked indigenous people, never owned slaves." And, yes. Not one of us was here when this house was built. Our immediate ancestors may have had nothing to do with it, but here we are, the current occupants of the property with stress cracks and bowed walls and fissures built into the foundation. We are the heirs to whatever is right or wrong with it. We did not erect the uneven pillars or joists, but they are ours to deal with now.

And any further deterioration is, in fact, on our hands. Unaddressed, the ruptures and diagonal cracks will not fix themselves. The toxins will not go away but, rather, will spread, leech, and mutate as they already have. When people live in an old house, they come to adjust to the idiosyncrasies and outright dangers skulking in an old structure. They put buckets under a wet ceiling, prop up groaning floors, learn to step over that rotting wood tread in the staircase. The awkward becomes acceptable, and the unacceptable becomes merely inconvenient. Live with it long enough, and the unthinkable becomes normal. Exposed over the generations, we learn to believe that the incomprehensible is the way that life is supposed to be.[18]

The trite responses to sin the world offers have found a cozy home within too many churches. Rugged individualism has been theologically constructed as a shield warding off all responsibility to deal with the structural damage in our "old house." Many Christians not only deny any responsibility to address all preexisting structural damage to our "old house" but also insist that they have no biblical mandate to repent of the sins of their ancestors. These members of the body commonly balk at pursuing needed change beyond prayer. But while prayer is imperative and must serve as our starting point and something we continue to engage in without ceasing, it cannot be our exhaustive response to injustice and systemic sin. Repentance is required, for our sins and the sins of our ancestors.

Biblically, corporate sin involves enforcing and adhering to sinful laws that explicitly oppose God's will and harm our neighbors. Corporate sin is more than active participation in sin; it includes apathy and complicity, or failing to act, in the face of evil amid oppressive contexts. Many Christian traditions thus include liturgical prayers for God's forgiveness for both the things we have done and the things we have left undone.

Scripture repeatedly addresses corporate sin, ranging from xenophobia to the enslavement of one's neighbor, the creation of ethnic caste systems that privilege some and disenfranchise others, the extortion of the least of these, infanticide, and idolatry. We see the Bible addressing these kinds of corporate sin in the empires of Babylon (Dan. 3), Egypt (Ex. 1:6–22), Persia (Est. 3), and Rome (Matt. 2). And God explicitly indicts Israel for their participation and complicity in corporate sin (Mic. 6) because it violates the covenant they made with God (Ex. 19:3–6, 10–12; Deut. 4:6–8).

Scripture also consistently ties corporate sin to generational sin.

- Israel corporately gathered to confess and connect its spiritual condition to its corporate complicity with sin and the sins of its ancestors (Neh. 9).
- The psalmist addressed culpability for the sins of Israel's ancestors: "Both we and our fathers have sinned; we have committed iniquity; we have done wickedness" (Ps. 106:6 ESV).
- God spoke to generational sin, saying, "Because of their iniquity, and also because of the iniquities of their fathers they shall rot away like them. But if they confess their iniquity and the iniquity of their fathers in their treachery that they committed against me . . . then I will remember my covenant with Jacob" (Lev. 26:39–42 ESV).
- Jeremiah connected corporate and generational sin, explaining that God required Israel not only to acknowledge their own wickedness but also their ancestors' sins (Jer. 3:25; 14:20).

- Isaiah spoke to corporate sin, declaring that he lived "in the midst of a people of unclean lips" and warned that the Lord would repay "both your iniquities and your father's iniquities together" (Isa. 6:5; 65:7 ESV).
- Ezekiel linked corporate and generational sin when he told Israel to confront "the detestable practices of their ancestors" (Ezek. 20:4). Most of the chapter focuses on the judgment on Israel because of the sin and unfaithfulness of their ancestors.

Countercultural Love

When the people of God refuse to address the sins of our ancestors and the privileges their sins continue to systemically imbue, we also forsake Jesus' instruction: "I give you a new commandment, that you love one another. Just as I have loved you, you also should love one another. By this everyone will know that you are my disciples, if you have love for one another" (John 13:34–35 NRSV). When we choose not to address inequities that we know infringe upon the shalom God created all people to enjoy and ignore privileges that sustain ungodly inequities, we miss out on precious opportunities to bear witness to our faith in Christ by failing to sacrificially love one another the way Jesus first loved us.

Furthermore, how we love one another is not just a matter of justice; it is a matter of evangelism. Scripture says that if we love one another well, people will identify us as Jesus' disciples, and through identifying and experiencing God's love in and through us, many will come to know God themselves. Therefore, how we love our neighbor not only bears witness to who and whose we are but to God's character and nature. Love thus becomes a defining marker of Christian identity, especially amid a polarized world where most people are unwilling to sacrificially love one another, especially across lines of difference.

The gospel declares that followers of Jesus are called to be a set-apart people with a radically alternative ethical mandate and vision of belonging. Instead of affirming the age-old adage "Blood is thicker than water," Scripture reveals that the baptismal waters are actually thicker than our biological bloodlines, and therefore declares that baptism—not DNA—redefines who our family is as the people of God. This gospel definition of family commissions us into the world as colaborers with Christ who are partnering to reconcile the world—broken people like you and me but also broken systems and structures—back to God. This means that followers of Christ are no longer able to respond to brokenness like the rest of the world.

The divisions that continue to disjoint the body of Christ and destabilize our "old house" are a consequence of unrepentant sin and hard-heartedness. We are too unwilling to confess the church's culpability in corporate sin and to acknowledge how our ancestors' sins continue to plague our land. Yet Christ calls us to do the hard work of curating a common memory that soberly articulates how systemic injustice and unrepentant sin have distorted Christian ethics and discipleship in ways that obstruct justice and infringe on the communion we were created to enjoy together.

The gospel is costly, and too many Christians have forgotten this biblical truth. Salvadoran archbishop Óscar Romero—whose faithful witness cost him his life—wrote, "The church must suffer for speaking the truth, for pointing out sin, for uprooting sin. No one wants to have a sore spot touched, and therefore a society with so many sores twitches when someone has the courage to touch it and say: 'You have to treat that. You have to get rid of that. Believe in Christ. Be converted.'"[19] Today we find ourselves in such a moment. We live in a time when we, too, must suffer for speaking the truth, pointing out the systemic sins plaguing our nation and committing ourselves to uprooting them.

Getting into Good Trouble

While many Christians have been discipled to think of justice as a secular issue, it is a matter of Christian discipleship. Not only is advocating for justice in an oppressive context biblical, but the prophet Micah reminds us that it is what the Lord requires of us. However, our theology has been tainted by our individualistic culture, which says we only have to be concerned about injustice when it directly impacts us, those we love, or those we see ourselves as connected to, but the gospel proclaims a profoundly different truth. The gospel declares that we are inherently connected to one another, and that our individual freedom, flourishing, and prosperity are tied to communal thriving. Within the realm of the kingdom, we collectively experience liberation and shalom, and we do so by seeking the peace and prosperity of our neighbors and taking on a Christlike mindset.

One of the reasons corporate sin is such a misunderstood biblical concept is because many congregations continue to have a surface-level reading of Romans 13:1–7, which emboldens a blind allegiance to law and order. But legal power does not equate to ethical power. Many governing authorities refuse to reflect God's heart and actively oppose the will of God in their governance.

New Testament scholar Esau McCaulley addresses how this passage has been misinterpreted and weaponized against Christians striving to serve as colaborers with Christ, reconciling the world to God. McCaulley writes that Paul's instruction to submit to governing authorities must be read in light of "Paul's use of Pharaoh *in Romans* as an example of God removing authorities through human agents shows that his prohibition against resistance is not absolute" and "the wider Old Testament testifies to God's use of human agents to take down corrupt governments."[20]

McCaulley argues that "Paul grounds his call for submission to the state with a description of what the state should do."[21] McCaulley anchors his interpretation of Paul in Romans 13:3–4, which reads, "For rulers are not a terror to good conduct, but to bad. Do you wish to have no fear of the authority? Then do what is good, and you will receive its approval; for it is God's servant for your good. But if you do what is wrong, you should be afraid, for the authority does not bear the sword in vain! It is the servant of God to execute wrath on the wrongdoer" (NRSV).

Given that Paul says that the innocent should not have to fear law enforcement or its government, McCaulley states, "This problem of innocent fearfulness continues to plague encounters between Black persons and law enforcement."[22] He then explains that "Paul does not focus on individual actions [of law enforcement], but on power structures."[23] These nuances lead McCaulley to conclude,

For the American Christian this means that he or she has to face the fact that our government has crafted laws over the course of centuries, not decades, that were designed to disenfranchise Black people. These laws were then enforced by means of the state's power of the sword. Historically in America, the issue has been institutional corporate sin undergirded by the policing power of the state.[24]

Few Christians understood this truth like Martin Luther King Jr. He addressed how governing authority can actively oppose the will of God in his "Letter from a Birmingham Jail," saying, "Never forget that everything Hitler did in Germany was legal." He continued, "One has not only a legal, but a moral responsibility to obey just laws. Conversely, one has a moral responsibility to disobey unjust laws."[25] Christians formed and shaped by Dr. King and pastors from a Kingian legacy frequently subscribe to an Augustinian logic that professes, "An unjust law is no law at all."[26]

Augustine profoundly shaped Dr. King's thinking. King ultimately determined, "An individual who breaks a law that conscience tells him is unjust, and who willingly accepts the penalty of imprisonment to arouse the conscience of the community over its injustice, is in reality expressing the highest respect for the law."[27] Interpreting Scripture as legitimizing nonviolent civil disobedience has been a major ecclesial dividing line, despite biblical precedent for this interpretation (Ex. 1:18–22; 2:2–3; Dan. 3).

In a sermon titled "A Knock at Midnight," given in 1963, Dr. King declared, "The church must be reminded that it is not the master or the servant of the state, but rather the conscience of the state. It must be the guide and the critic of the state, and never its tool. If the church does not recapture its prophetic zeal, it will become an irrelevant social club without moral or spiritual authority."[28] His faithful comrade John Lewis left us with instructions for living into King's charge. At a speech given on the Edmund Pettus Bridge three months before his death, Lewis proclaimed, "Get in good trouble, necessary trouble, and help redeem the soul of America."[29]

Remembrance, Faithfulness, and Repentance

A clear foundational connection exists between identity and remembrance in Scripture. Consequently, the ahistorical nature of our theology is another of the primary challenges before us. To heal the transgressions that fracture the body and destabilize our "old house," we must remember, confess, lament, and produce fruit in keeping with repentance by turning away from our sins of omission and commission. One reason we have forsaken the spiritual practice of lament is because we have failed to heed Scripture's call to remember. When we do not remember, lament seems unwarranted, pursuing justice seems optional, and the vital work of curating a common memory is forsaken.

As the church, we are called to reclaim remembrance as a spiritual practice. In the Old Testament alone, God instructs Israel to remember approximately one hundred times. Remembrance was the linchpin for Israel's faithfulness. When Israel remembered, they were a faithful witness. When Israel remembered, they lived out of thanksgiving. They acknowledged that God freed them from slavery and called them to be a distinct people, set apart. God instructed Israel to live out of this remembrance, and as a fruit of their remembrance, Israel was not to exploit migrant workers but to pay fair wages, not to deprive the foreigner or the fatherless of justice but to ensure that they made provisions for the poor, widows, and orphans. But when Israel forgot, they were just as prone to participate in or acquiesce to corporate sin as any other people and nation. When they failed to remember who they were and whose they were, Israel created unjust systems and structures (Mic. 6) that exploited the poor and the needy, and they mistook their chosen-ness as God always blessing whatever they did, even when they were covenantally unfaithful.

We, too, have failed to remember, and this failure has led too many believers to cling to unbiblical responses to sin. In the face of grotesque injustices and lingering disparities that are the direct by-products of sinful legislation, too many Christians remain apathetic and indifferent. Rather than downplaying corporate and generational sin or trying to absolve ourselves from the responsibility of partnering with God as ambassadors of reconciliation—which includes restoring not only broken people but also broken systems and structures to God—Christians should be leading the way in this pivotal moment.

Reflection Questions

1. How can we corporately repent for the unrelenting onslaught against the sanctity of Black life?
2. Where do you see corporate sin today?

3. How do passages like Nehemiah 9 and Jeremiah 3:25; 14:20 help us think more biblically about corporate and generational sin?
4. How does Esau McCaulley's scholarship on Romans 13 shift how you interpret that passage?
5. How is getting into good, necessary trouble connected to Scripture's call to leverage privilege to further the kingdom and love our neighbors?
6. How can remembrance become a spiritual practice of accountability?

CHAPTER 9

PRODUCING FRUIT IN KEEPING WITH REPENTANCE

When we go to the doctor, he or she will not begin to treat us without taking our history—and not just our history but that of our parents and grandparents before us. The doctor will not see us until we have filled out many pages on a clipboard that is handed to us upon arrival. The doctor will not hazard a diagnosis until he or she knows the history going back generations.

As we fill out the pages of our medical past, and our current complaints, what our bodies have been exposed to and what they have survived, it does us no good to pretend that certain ailments have not beset us, to deny the full truths of what brought us to this moment. Few problems have ever been solved by ignoring them.

> *Looking beneath the history of one's*
> *country is like learning that alcoholism or*
> *depression runs in one's family or that suicide*
> *has occurred more often than might be usual*
> *or, with the advances in medical genetics*
> *discovering that one has inherited the markers*
> *of a BRCA mutation for breast cancer. You*
> *don't ball up in a corner with guilt or shame*
> *at these discoveries. You don't, if you are wise,*
> *forbid any mention of them. In fact, you do*
> *the opposite. You educate yourself. You talk*
> *to people who have been through it and to*
> *specialists who have researched it. You learn*
> *the consequences and obstacles, the options and*
> *treatment. You may pray over it and meditate*
> *over it. Then you take precautions to protect*
> *yourself and succeeding generations and work*
> *to ensure that these things, whatever they are,*
> *don't happen again.*
>
> —Isabel Wilkerson, *Caste: The*
> *Origins of Our Discontents*[1]

Subversive witnesses must confront the truth, no matter how difficult it is to do so. We must then speak the truth to our neighbors and family members, in our congregations and community, and to the powers that be. Scripture gives us a framework in which to do this. We have the spiritual practices needed—remembrance, confession, lament, and repentance—to ensure that the sins of our ancestors are never repeated. We also have the biblical mandate to serve as colaborers with Christ and ambassadors of reconciliation. We have a model in Jesus and an advocate in the Holy Spirit who empowers us to partner with Jesus as his hands and feet in the world, ushering in the inbreaking kingdom by producing fruit in keeping with repentance and rectifying the ways sin has perverted systems, structures, and laws in the world.

Producing fruit in keeping with repentance requires moral clarity, spiritual maturity, sacrificial love, and humility. We cultivate this Christlike posture by steadfastly praying Psalm 139:23–24 (KJV), "Search me, O God, and know my heart: try me, and know my thoughts: and see if there be any wicked way in me, and lead me in the way everlasting." This prayer illuminates our complicity, conformity to this world, and need for repentance. This prayer teaches us to walk humbly with God, and as we learn, the Spirit moves to renew our minds, showing us how to love mercy, do justice, and offer our bodies as living sacrifices to God.

Unbridled Privilege

When unchecked, privilege distorts how we see God, our neighbor, ourselves, and creation. It also perverts how we read the Bible and live out our faith. It lures us into interpreting challenging Scripture passages as optional or only applicable to others.

The free will God grants us is easily corrupted by privilege. When this occurs, our ethics erode, our love is domesticated, and our witness is destroyed. Scripture is clear: the devil's sole purpose is to kill, steal, and destroy. Satan uses unbridled privilege as a vehicle for this mission. When we succumb to the temptation to exploit privilege, we disobey Jesus' commandment to love one another as he first loved us. In our disobedience, we miss out on prime opportunities to share God's love, reconcile divisions, and demonstrate that we are Jesus' disciples to the world.

For example, privilege has seduced too many Christians with US citizenship into believing the gospel gives us the choice of welcoming, resisting, or expelling the stranger among us. Evangelical leaders Jenny Yang and Matthew Soerens write that the Hebrew word *ger* is "the most common word, and that which best describes the immigrant we encounter . . . strangers who establish themselves, at least for a time, in a foreign land." They add, "The noun *ger* alone appears ninety-two times in the Old Testament. Throughout the text, we find stories of *ger* (sojourners or immigrants), as well as guidance and commands from God to his people about how to treat the immigrants living among us."[2]

Yang and Soerens explore in detail what the Bible says about immigration and conclude, "God does not suggest that we welcome immigrants; he commands it—not once or twice, but over and over again."[3] This is not to say there are not valid and vital questions that must be addressed regarding immigration reform and what it entails, but it does mean that too many Christians are using sources other than Scripture as the foundation for their beliefs and civic engagement regarding immigration. This was exemplified by a 2015 poll that revealed that only 12 percent of evangelical Christians said the Bible was their primary influence for thinking about immigration.

Moreover, unexamined privilege entices many Christians

to read passages like Matthew 25 as merely a list of good suggestions to pick and choose from rather than a comprehensive biblical commission given by our Lord and Savior. Consequently, many believers may feed the hungry, provide drink for the thirsty, and clothe needy neighbors at a local shelter but never visit the incarcerated, welcome the stranger, or look after nonrelatives who are sick. While we are called to compassion, mercy, and justice, privilege makes too many Christians content with neglecting the weightier matters of justice.[4]

Unbridled privilege emboldens an *a la carte* faith that masquerades as Christianity. It leads us to believe we can truly serve two masters, that we can follow Jesus and retain control over our lives rather than dying to self so that Christ can rise and live in and through us. It tempts Christians into believing that justice is something some members of the body are "called to" or "passionate about." It inhibits a liturgy that bears witness to the fact that all believers are called to be colaborers with Christ in proclaiming good news to the poor, freedom for the prisoners, and recovery of sight for the blind, and in setting the oppressed free. Partnering with Christ in this manner is inconvenient, uncomfortable, and costly. It requires becoming proximate to the least of these, engaging in advocacy and activism as expressions of love for our neighbors, and calling for institutional accountability on local, state, and federal levels.

The Spirit of the Lord Is upon Us

The Spirit of the Lord is upon us, compelling us to pursue shalom amid worldly empires. Robert Chao Romero writes that the "holistic focus of the good news is referred to by the Brown

Theologians as *misión integral*."[5] René Padilla defines *misión integral* as "the mission of the whole church to the whole of humanity in all its forms, personal, communal, social, economic, ecological, and political."[6] This is the work of the church, the liturgy Scripture calls us to pursue.

Those of us with the privilege and power of citizenship are called to see and exercise our citizenship as a vehicle for collective liberation. Citizenship is a status that endows power, and this power should be exerted to further the kingdom and pursue justice. Willie Jennings writes,

> The church constantly forgets that it must see citizenship from this position, because this was the position of our savior, who felt the force of empire on his own body. Instead, we too often imagine citizenship from the privileged position of options. We have in many times and places imagined we have options—to become involved in politics or not, to concern ourselves with contentious issues or not, to advocate for people or not, to claim our citizenship or not, or to speak out or remain silent.[7]

The life of Jesus demonstrates that these "options" are not faithful to our calling.

Citizenship is a tool we wield to expose systemic sin, overturn imperial injustice, and defend the dignity of the disinherited. Jennings explains, "The purpose of citizenship for a disciple of Jesus is to use the emperor's gold to break the emperor's hold on lives and to use the systems that construct pawns [those satiated by empire] to shatter the chains of servitude." He continues, "Citizenship represents the constrained conditions within which disciples must work, knowing that the only political position we should take is one calibrated to the goal of announcing the redemption of creaturely life, and the overturning of all that which would destroy God's creation."[8] Living in this manner acknowledges that the gospel is political but is not partisan.

To participate in the inbreaking kingdom amid worldly empires with anti-gospel priorities, principles, and values is political. We must not be afraid to be political, but our political action must be submitted to and guided by the Holy Spirit. Jennings writes, "The incarnate life of God was life lived inside our political spaces, and from within those spaces God announced the divine reign and the emergence of a new citizenship, the citizenship of heaven. The disciple-citizen lives then in this new citizenship that makes intelligible their actions in the worldly republics they inhabit. We are citizens of heaven first, born anew into a living hope."[9] How we understand and exercise our citizenship—and the privileges it affords—declares what we pledge allegiance to.

We must live in a manner that bears witness to God's will here on earth as it is in heaven. And as Jennings concludes, "Our actions inside worldly republics must be calibrated by this citizenship that reaches far beyond the hopes of any nation-state, any tribal-nation, or corporation (Phil. 3:20–21)."[10] We can only live like this when the Spirit of the Lord is upon us.

As subversive witnesses, the Spirit of God leads us into uncharted territory and compels us to love people we would never choose to love on our own. The Spirit brings life out of death and leads us into perilous spaces to seek the kingdom first in revolutionary ways. The Holy Spirit is untamed and will lead us to do uncomfortable and cruciform things. The

Spirit of God may inspire you to step out in faith to do the following:

- Break an unjust law like the Hebrew midwives did.
- Risk your familial inheritance to end generational cycles of bigotry and hatred that have enslaved your family for far too long, like Pharaoh's daughter did.
- Endure incarceration for resisting exploitation and affirming your dignity, like Queen Vashti did.
- Reconnect to the suffering of your people and risk your life for their freedom, like Esther did.
- Confront the powers that be to demand God's people be freed, pursuing collective liberation over your individual freedom, like Moses did.
- Endure economic, social, and/or political persecution for bearing witness to the inbreaking kingdom amid an oppressive worldly empire with other priorities, like Jesus did.
- Speak truth to power, proclaiming good news to the poor, freedom for the prisoners, recovery of sight for the blind, and freedom for the oppressed in accordance with the year of the Lord's favor, like Jesus did.
- Stand in solidarity with your oppressed neighbors to expose systemic sin and demand institutional account-ability and reform in our criminal justice—as well as our education, health care, immigration, and judicial—system and government, like Paul and Silas did.
- Give half of your possessions to the poor, and provide reparations to those you come to realize you have exploited through your vocation—or that your ancestors exploited

to establish a family fortune—as a fruit of your repentance, like Zacchaeus did.

These are not choices these men and women made in their own strength. The Spirit of the Lord was upon them, and that same Spirit is drawing us out of our comfort zones into unfamiliar spaces where our faith will be tested and our neighbors' greatest needs exist. When we submit to the Spirit and follow Jesus' example, our sacrificial love will change the world.

When I interviewed Bryan Stevenson, I asked him about the courage and long-suffering it takes to constantly choose this nature of unrelenting sacrificial love. He said,

> The good news is that it's not a new struggle. People of faith and people of conviction have always had to stand up when other people say sit down and to speak when other people say to be quiet. And you get oriented to live like that, to think like that, to believe like that. I'm a product of a community where people were marginalized, poor, excluded. We had to learn to believe things we hadn't seen, and my faith reinforced that.[11]

Elsewhere, Stevenson explains, "We cannot create justice without getting close to places where injustices prevail."[12] He also says,

> We are going to have to do things that are uncomfortable and inconvenient, because we do not change the world by only doing the things that are comfortable and convenient. And I hate that, because we're humans, and humans are

biologically and psychologically programed to do what's comfortable. We like comfort. And that means that we are going to have to make a choice to do uncomfortable things.[13]

The Spirit empowers us to make this uncomfortable and inconvenient choice.

The Fast God Desires

When Jesus proclaimed his mission statement in Luke 4:18–19, he referenced Isaiah 58. In this passage, God indicts Israel yet again for their covenantal infidelity. Israel has forgotten who and whose they are. Old Testament scholar Walter Brueggemann writes, "The term 'delight' ('to know my ways'; v. 2), the term for 'delight' ('to draw near'; v. 2), and the term 'interest' (v. 3) are all the same Hebrew term *hps*." Brueggemann then explains, "What has happened is that *self-interest* and *God's delight* have gotten confused and are identified with each other. The outcome of such a distorted religion that conceals self-interest . . . [is] an attack on religious practice that is excessively utilitarian, serving one's own interests."[14]

The self-serving "fast" of Israel provided the context for the rest of the chapter, particularly verses 6–9, where we read about the nature of fasting God desires.

> "Is not this the kind of fasting I have chosen:
>   to loose the chains of injustice
>   and untie the cords of the yoke,
>   to set the oppressed free
>   and break every yoke?

Is it not to share your food with the hungry
and to provide the poor wanderer with shelter—
when you see the naked, to clothe them,
and not to turn away from your own flesh and blood?
Then your light will break forth like the dawn,
and your healing will quickly appear;
then your righteousness will go before you,
and the glory of the LORD will be your rear guard.
Then you will call, and the LORD will answer;
you will cry for help, and he will say: Here am I."

Israel, amid exploiting all their workers, purported to humbly fast while infighting—"striking each other with wicked fists"—and wondered why God did not hear their voice. God responded by calling Israel to repent and produce fruit in keeping with repentance. God commissioned Israel to end injustice, oppression, and exploitation. God then decreed that Israel would be answered when they leveraged what they had been entrusted with to further the kingdom and love their neighbors—particularly their most vulnerable neighbors: the hungry, the poor, and the naked.

The Bible commonly links justice to taking care of and taking up the cause of "the least of these" (widows, orphans, immigrants, and the poor). The Hebrew word for "justice" is *mishpat*. It occurs more than two hundred times in the Old Testament. *Mishpat* involves advocating on behalf of, caring for, and protecting the most vulnerable members of society. Old Testament professor Donald Gowan writes, "The *mishpat*, or justness, of a society, according to the Bible, is evaluated by how it treats these groups. Any neglect shown to the needs of the members of this quartet is not called merely a lack of mercy or charity but a violation of justice, of *mishpat*. God loves and defends those with the least economic and social power, and so should we. That is what it means to 'do justice.'"[15]

Scripture illustrates that the people of God are held accountable by God when they fail to do justice. When Israel neglected their responsibility to do justice and care for the least of these, they were sent into exile or rebuked by God-ordained prophets, or God refused to hear and receive their "worship" because it was self-centered.

God reprimanded Israel for their disobedience. Brueggemann writes that the fast the Lord requires is "moral passion under discipline for the things of God . . . a hands-on assault on injustice. The issues are focused exclusively on economic matters, which ask the community to step outside its self-interest to focus on the other."[16] Israel created such an unjust society that the only way the least of these would ever be liberated from economic bondage was if Israel moved to set the captives free by undoing the economic exploitation it created in rebellion and defiance of God. Israel therefore had deceived themselves into believing that their idolatry and oppression were fasting, worship of God as opposed to worship of self. In the same manner that Israel perverted fasting, we have adulterated repentance.

Let's Get Free

Repentance is about freedom from sin. It liberates us to freely and fully follow Jesus, to make God's love known and shown, fulfilling the Great Commission and the Greatest Commandment.

To leverage privilege to further the kingdom, love our neighbors, and pursue collective liberation, we will also have to be liberated from sinful ideologies that bind us. Like Jesus, we will have to overturn some oppressive tables. A few of the anti-gospel tables we will have to overturn—not an exhaustive list—as subversive witnesses include rugged individualism, white supremacy, and patriarchy. A freer life, an abundant life in Christ is awaiting us when we cast down these idols and embrace the collective liberation the gospel affords.

Theologian Wendell Berry, in his prophetic book *The Hidden Wound*, writes about the captivity of rugged individualism:

> Our present idea of freedom is only the freedom to do as we please: to sell ourselves for a high salary, a home in the suburbs, and idle weekends. But that is a freedom dependent upon affluence, which is in turn dependent upon the rapid consumption of exhaustible supplies. The other kind of freedom is the freedom to take care of ourselves and of each other. The freedom of affluence opposes and contradicts the freedom of community life.[17]

We were created for so much more; the gospel calls us into a sacred mutuality that is exclusively realized in Christ.

Theologian Drew Hart cautions us not to confuse the "freedom" of rugged individualism with divine liberation. "Our belief that freedom means the ability to do whatever we want, or the agency to accomplish whatever we desire, is flawed; it refuses to account for our responsibility to the flourishing of all humanity as a beloved community." He then concludes, "It also ignores how deeply our desires are already captive to much greater forces. We should not conflate American rights with God's righteousness, nor should we confuse American freedom for God's deliverance."[18]

One of the primary forces that precludes us from pursuing collective liberation is white supremacy. On May 31, 1965—less than two months after Bloody Sunday—Martin Luther King Jr. returned to Selma to speak about the future of the movement. At Brown Chapel, he spoke about what it would take to pursue collective liberation:

> We can't save the soul of America without in the process saving our white brothers. And they aren't free. When you enslave an individual, you enslave yourself. I mean all white brothers are slaves to that fear—slaves to their prejudices. How many white preachers are there in this town? Slaves to their congregations and they're afraid to take a stand and so they prefer to remain silent behind the safe security of stained-glass windows. They know that segregation is wrong. They know that they should take a stand but they are not free. They are afraid, and they haven't allowed the gospel of Jesus Christ to permeate their lives. And we've got to save those preachers. We have got to put Christianity in the church.[19]

While our fight is no longer about integration or the ability to register to vote, we are still fighting white supremacy and the death, oppression, and division it engenders. Ephesians 6:12 makes it clear: "Our struggle is not against flesh and blood, but against the rulers, against the authorities, against the powers of this dark world and against the spiritual forces of evil in the heavenly realms." Our fight is not against white people but against the demonic spirit of white supremacy. White supremacy is antithetical to the gospel in every way, shape, and form. It contradicts the biblical truth of Genesis 1:27 that we are all equitably made in God's image; engenders sin in systems, structures, laws, and the enforcement of laws; and functions as a tool Satan effectively uses to destroy the communion God created us to enjoy together.

Because Satan is the father of lies, all throughout the world there are still preachers who are not free. Not free to proclaim the gospel unadulterated, declaring that one cannot faithfully follow Jesus and subscribe to white supremacy. These preachers are enslaved to fear—afraid of being fired for speaking out against racism because their congregants resist discipleship that will exorcise the demon of white supremacy, afraid to have to address their own sin, and afraid of the cost of speaking this unpopular truth. Fifty-five years after King's sermon, we are still struggling "to put Christianity in the church."

We can no longer claim to fight for freedom when our movements force women of color to choose which part of their identity they will advocate for and which part they will silence. As Chanequa Walker-Barnes writes,

> Racial reconciliation's failure to interrogate patriarchy means that it will frequently reproduce the subordination of women. To put it bluntly, much of what passes for racial reconciliation among Christians is merely an exercise in making sure Black men and other men of color have the same access to male privilege as their White counterparts do. Racism and sexism, after all, have the same ultimate aim.[20]

We must renounce this counterfeit vision of freedom. We are not free when our sisters of color must choose between resisting racism or patriarchy because our congregations and freedom movements are not ready to address both. People are not ready for both because we have not prepared them to address both within our discipleship and leadership development pathways. As we continue to address racism and white supremacy, we must stop treating patriarchy as a secondary sin. We must begin addressing sexual violence, intimate partner violence, and rape culture within the spaces God has entrusted us to steward, be they churches, nonprofits, campuses, or camp settings.

Collectivist liberation means we can no longer be content with a pursuit of life together that gives patriarchy a pass by not holding men accountable for our actions, tolerating partial interpretations of difficult biblical texts, or condoning "locker room talk" within our midst. We must also find new ways to invest in called and gifted women within our sphere that do not force them to lead as men do and that affirm the vital insights that emerge from their lived experiences. We need to seek out established women leaders and sit at their feet to learn from their knowledge and wisdom. And we need to confess that it is a privilege to be merely drive-by advocates for our sisters, selectively addressing male privilege when it is convenient or not too costly. Our sisters deserve better and the gospel demands more.

The Cure Is in the Pain

Eighteen days after George Floyd's life was taken, Rayshard Brooks was unnecessarily killed by Garrett Rolfe, a police officer in Atlanta, Georgia. Louie Giglio, a megachurch pastor in Atlanta, tried to respond pastorally in the wake of the civil unrest. He convened a conversation on race relations, inviting two-time Grammy Award–winning artist Lecrae Moore and Chick-fil-A chief executive Dan Cathy to participate in a prerecorded conversation. During the conversation, Giglio said,

> We understand the curse that was slavery, white people do. And we say, that was bad, but we miss the blessing of slavery, that it actually built up the framework for the world that white people live in and lived in. And, so a lot of people call this white privilege, and when you say those two words, it just is like a fuse goes off for a lot of white people, because they don't want somebody telling them to check their privilege.[21]

Then Giglio said, in what I can only assume was an attempt at offering ministerial advice, "If the phrase [white privilege] is the trip up, let's get over the phrase, and let's get down to the heart. Let's get down to 'what then do you want to call it?' And I think maybe a great thing for me, is to call it 'white blessing.'"[22] Giglio was appropriately reprimanded by Black clergy and members of the body for his flagrant word choice, because in catering to white comfort, he spiritually abused the rest of the body and likely turned many people seeking answers away from desiring a relationship with God. Giglio later apologized on Twitter and in a video posted to social media, saying that he wants to help other white Christians understand the reality of white privilege and acknowledging that he has much to learn about racial justice.

I share this story not to pile on to Giglio's criticism, but to illustrate why it is so imperative to recognize that the cure for the pain is in the pain. We won't find genuine freedom without developing the courage and fortitude to soberly confront sin, access its deadly impact, and return to right(eous) relationship with God and neighbor. Followers of Christ must realize that we cannot crucify what we cannot name. When the church side-steps naming sin or uses adulterated allegories and metaphors to make sin more palatable, our response to sin will always be insufficient. As Pastor Richard A. Villodas Jr., lead pastor of New Life Fellowship, explained in his response to Louie Giglio's comments, we empower sin to establish a foothold within the body when we do not forthrightly name and renounce it.

Villodas wrote, "I'm consistently reminded of the deep challenge many have in using a phrase like white supremacy/privilege."[23] Referring to Voldemort, the chief antagonist in the Harry Potter books, whose name characters feared to speak out loud, Villodas concluded,

> Many people would rather refer to white supremacy/white privilege as "You know What" or "That-Which-Must-Not-Be-Named." But if you can't name it, you're still under its power. . . . The purpose of using terms like "white supremacy" is not to demonize others. It's to accurately name the history and the continual residue of that history in our day. I know these terms are difficult to speak for some, but unless we face them head-on, we will tip-toe around an issue that requires a powerful exorcism.[24]

Explicitly naming sin, especially transgressions that have remained afoot for centuries without being authentically addressed, is scary for many. Exposing and denouncing deeply rooted sins that are melded into the DNA of our nation and the Western church requires spiritual maturity, an embrace of the cost of discipleship, and a deep trust that God is truly who Scripture reveals our Creator to be. The Spirit will guide, refine, and sustain us amid these difficult conversations, but we must trust God's sufficiency by pressing into them. While many believers resist these conversations, labeling them as divisive, true division emanates from our tolerance of sin and refusal to address it.

When racial tragedies strike, they illuminate how ill-equipped most churches are to respond. Despite the enduring legacy of Black life being violently taken and the frequency with which it occurs, far too many Christians remain unprepared to respond in a fruitful manner. Too many believers lack a vision for faithful participation in the inbreaking kingdom.

Pastors who cower before imperial power and white discomfort must own their share of the blame because they fail to cast a gospel vision for their members. They fail to make disciples who desire to participate in biblical justice and are equipped to engage in a Spirit-filled righteous resistance against the powers, principalities, and spiritual wickedness that oppose the will of God. Pastors cannot allow the gospel we proclaim to be dictated by what our members are ready for on their own. We are called to lead and disciple, not placate, our members.

We must pursue a collective liberation that refuses to silence, marginalize, or subjugate others. We must pursue a vison of life together that keeps us from turning a blind eye to violence against our neighbors, whether it be violence enacted against the transgender community, sexual assault and domestic violence occurring within our own congregation, or the dehumanizing violence enacted within our criminal justice system. We also need a vision of freedom that calls us to ecological justice, in which we fight environmental racism, protect natural resources, and engage in sustainable consumption. Creation is groaning because of our sinful abuse, and we can no longer afford to fight for freedom in silos. We must cast a vision of liberation that truly breaks the chains of injustice and sets the oppressed free, and that is truly and tangibly good news to the least of these whose backs are against the wall.

Reflection Questions

1. What does it mean to keep with repentance?
2. How can we access the fruit of our repentance?
3. How can those of us who possess the privilege of citizenship leverage it to further the kingdom and sacrificially love our neighbors without citizenship?
4. What happens when we read challenging texts as good suggestions to pick and choose from rather than as biblical commissions? Can you think of a passage where you or your congregation do this?
5. Why is it good news that the people of God are held accountable by God when they fail to do justice?
6. Scripture calls us to speak the truth in love, but the rhetoric of love cannot shroud hard truths. So how do we soberly yet humbly address patriarchy and sexual violence, racism and white supremacy, and systemic and corporate sin in our country and congregations?

ACKNOWLEDGMENTS

I want to thank my parents and grandparents for sacrificing, struggling, and persevering more than I will ever fully understand to provide me with the opportunities I have been blessed with.

I want to thank my wife, Katherine, for her unwavering support. She grounds me. She helps me heal in ways I didn't know I needed to, and her compassion and conviction expands our familial pursuit of life together with our disinherited neighbors.

I want to thank Jazzy Johnson for being an external content advisor for this project. This book literally would not be what it is without your voice, feedback, and insights. Thanks for processing with me, pushing me, and colaboring to help produce this project.

NOTES

Introduction

1. See Leviticus 19:9; 23:22; Judges 8:2; Ruth 2:23; et al.
2. See Leviticus 25:8–55.
3. "The Hellenistic Widows," Fuller, accessed January 18, 2021, https://www.fuller.edu/next-faithful-step/resources/the-hellenistic-widows/.
4. In *The Very Good Gospel*, Lisa Sharon Harper says that shalom is when all people have enough. She goes on to describe shalom as a movement of God breaking through, where all families are healed and when churches, schools, and public policies protect human dignity. Shalom, Harper explains, is when the image of God is recognized, protected, and cultivated in every single human. Shalom is our calling as followers of Jesus' gospel. It is the vision God set forth in the garden and the restoration God desires for every broken relationship. Shalom is what our souls long for. Shalom is the "very good" in the gospel. Harper, *The Very Good Gospel: How Everything Wrong Can Be Made Right* (Colorado Springs: WaterBrook, 2016). For more, see https://lisasharonharper.com/the-very-good-gospel/.

Chapter 1: Understanding Privilege and Its Power

1. The word *Black* is capitalized through this book when referring to descendants from the African diaspora. When *Black* is used, it is intended to be inclusive of the African diaspora regardless of a person's affiliation with or connection to the United States. *Black* is also intended to connote the global phenomenon of anti-Black racism. Finally, capitalizing the *B* in *Black* is consistent with other capitalization standards, as in Native, Asian, and Latin Americans.

2. Errin Whack, "Who Was Edmund Pettus? The March to Freedom Started on a Bridge That Honors a Man Bent on Preserving Slavery and Segregation," *Smithsonian Magazine*, March 7, 2015, https://www.smithsonianmag.com/history /who-was-edmund-pettus-180954501/.

3. Whack, "Who Was Edmund Pettus?"

4. Whack, "Who Was Edmund Pettus?"

5. Whack, "Who Was Edmund Pettus?"

6. Whack, "Who Was Edmund Pettus?"

7. Whack, "Who Was Edmund Pettus?"

8. WSFA Staff, "Great-Great-Granddaughter of Edmund Pettus Wants Bridge Renamed," *NBC News*, July 26, 2020, https://www .nbc12.com/2020/07/26/great-great-granddaughter-edmund -pettus-wants-bridge-renamed/.

9. Bryan Stevenson, "Truth-Telling before Reconciliation: A Conversation with Bryan Stevenson," from a conversation between Bryan Stevenson and Michael Nilsen, August 31, 2017, AFP, January 1, 2018, https://afpglobal.org/news/truth -telling-reconciliation.

10. Stevenson, "Truth-Telling before Reconciliation."

11. Quoted in Marlene Brant Castellano, Linda Archibald, and Mike DeGagné, *From Truth to Reconciliation: Transforming the Legacy of Residential Schools* (Ottawa, ON: Aboriginal Healing Foundation, 2008), xviii, www.ahf.ca/downloads

/from-truth-to-reconciliation-transforming-the-legacy-of
-residential-schools.pdf.

12. Corey Turner, "Why America's Schools Have
    A Money Problem," NPR, April 18, 2016.
    https://www.npr.org/2016/04/18/474256366/why
    -americas-schools-have-a-money-problem.

13. Nonwhite school districts included many large cities and were
    much larger than the white districts. White school districts
    included many small rural areas. "Nonwhite School Districts
    Get $23 Billion Less Than White Districts Despite Serving the
    Same Number of Students," EdBuild, accessed January 18, 2021,
    https://edbuild.org/content/23-billion.

14. Laura Meckler, "Report Finds $23 Billion Racial
    Funding Gap for Schools," *Washington Post*, February
    25, 2019, https://www.washingtonpost.com/local
    /education/report-finds-23-billion-racial-funding-gap-for
    -schools/2019/02/25/d562b704-3915-11e9-a06c-3ec8ed509d15
    _story.html.

15. Meckler, "Report Finds $23 Billion Racial Funding Gap for
    Schools."

16. Twenty-seven percent of students are enrolled in
    predominantly nonwhite districts. Twenty-six percent of
    students are enrolled in predominantly white districts.

17. "Nonwhite School Districts Get $23 Billion Less," EdBuild.

18. "Race—The Power of an Illusion," PBS, accessed January 18, 2021,
    https://www.pbs.org/race/000_About/002_06_a-godeeper.htm.

19. Kimberlé Crenshaw, "Mapping the Margins: Intersectionality,
    Identity Politics, and Violence against Women of Color,"
    Stanford Law Review 43, no. 6 (July 1991).

20. Alan H. Goodman, Yolanda T. Moses, and Joseph L. Jones, *Race:
    Are We So Different?* (Hoboken: Wiley-Blackwell, 2012), 203.

21. *APA Dictionary of Psychology*, s.v. "ingroup bias," accessed
    January 18, 2021, https://dictionary.apa.org/ingroup-bias.

22. Okhee Park Hong, "A Cognitive Approach to the Study of Ingroup Bias: Role of Reasons," Iowa State University Digital Repository, 1988, https://lib.dr.iastate.edu/cgi/viewcontent .cgi?article=9771&context=rtd; Pascal Molenberghs and Winnifred R. Louis, "Insights from fMRI Studies into Ingroup Bias," *Frontiers in Psychology* 9 (October 1, 2018): 1868, doi:10.3389/fpsyg.2018.01868.

23. Marina Koren, "Telling the Story of the Stanford Rape Case," *The Atlantic*, June 6, 2016, https://www.theatlantic.com/news /archive/2016/06/stanford-sexual-assault-letters/485837/.

24. Daniel Victor, "Ethan Couch, 'Affluenza Teen' Who Killed 4 While Driving Drunk, Is Freed," *New York Times*, April 2, 2018, https://www.nytimes.com/2018/04/02/us/ethan-couch -affluenza-jail.html.

25. The Sentencing Project, "Report to the United Nations on Racial Disparities in the U.S. Criminal Justice System," April 19, 2018, https://www.sentencingproject.org/publications/un -report-on-racial-disparities/. This report was submitted to the United Nations Special Rapporteur on Contemporary Forms of Racism, Racial Discrimination, Xenophobia, and Related Intolerance.

26. "Death Penalty," Equal Justice Initiative, accessed January 18, 2021, https://eji.org/issues/death-penalty/.

27. "Race," Death Penalty Information Center, accessed January 18, 2021, https://deathpenaltyinfo.org/policy-issues/race.

28. Statistic comes from the Death Penalty Information Center. See https://deathpenaltyinfo.org/policy-issues/race/race -rape-and-the-death-penalty.

29. "Race," Death Penalty Information Center.

30. McCleskey v. Kemp, 481 U.S. 279, 312 (1987).

31. Dominique Gilliard, *Rethinking Incarceration: Advocating for Justice That Restores* (Downers Grove, IL: InterVarsity, 2018), 22.

32. The exception to this statement being someone who has sex reassignment surgery.

33. Billy Graham, "What's 'the Billy Graham Rule'?"
    Billy Graham Evangelistic Association, July
    23, 2019, https://billygraham.org/story/the
    -modesto-manifesto-a-declaration-of-biblical-integrity/.

Chapter 2: Pharaoh's Daughter

1. CSKC, INP, Coretta Scott King Collection, "In Private Hands,"
   sermon file folder 159, speeches, reprints in various magazines,
   M. L. King.
2. Terence E. Fretheim, *Exodus: Interpretation: A Bible
   Commentary for Teaching and Preaching* (Louisville:
   Westminster John Knox, 2010), 31.
3. While autonomy looks different within a theocratic monarchy,
   it still existed. And while it is dangerous to stand up for what
   is right amid an oppressive regime, over the course of time,
   people in many places and under a multitude of governments
   have sacrificed their own well-being for the common good in
   this manner. Consent to the powers that be, especially amid
   grievous injustice, is a choice, albeit a difficult one to make.
4. James Bruckner, *Exodus: New International Biblical
   Commentary* (Grand Rapids: Baker, 2008), 27.
5. Bruckner, *Exodus*, 27.
6. Fretheim, *Exodus*, 38.
7. Fretheim, *Exodus*, 38.
8. Bruckner, *Exodus*, 26.
9. Fretheim, *Exodus*, 38. Emphasis added.
10. Bruckner, *Exodus*, 22.
11. Bruckner, *Exodus*, 23.
12. Bruckner, *Exodus*, 26.

Chapter 3: Esther

1. Brenda Salter McNeil, *Becoming Brave: Finding the Courage to
   Pursue Racial Justice Now* (Grand Rapids: Brazos, 2020), 55.
2. McNeil, *Becoming Brave*, 55.

3. Bianca Mabute-Louie, "Queen Vashti: Identifying and Interrupting Toxic Masculinity," Inheritance, March 5, 2019, https://www.inheritancemag.com/stories/queen-vashti.

4. Jimmy Carter, "Women Live in a Profoundly Different, More Dangerous World," The Elders, November 25, 2013, https://www.theelders.org/news/women-live-profoundly-different-more-dangerous-world.

5. "Broken Silence: A Call for Churches to Speak Out: Protestant Pastors Survey on Sexual and Domestic Violence," Sojourners and IMA World Health, June 2014, https://imaworldhealth.org/wp-content/uploads/2014/07/PastorsSurveyReport_final1.pdf.

6. "Speech by Jimmy Carter to the Parliament of the World's Religions," Melbourne, AU, delivered via remote video from Atlanta, The Carter Center, December 2, 2009, https://www.cartercenter.org/news/editorials_speeches/parliament-world-religions-120309.html.

7. Kathy Khang, *Raise Your Voice: Why We Stay Silent and How to Speak Up* (Downers Grove, IL: InterVarsity, 2018), 24.

8. McNeil, *Becoming Brave*, 69.

9. Walter Brueggemann, *The Prophetic Imagination*, 2nd ed. (Minneapolis: Fortress, 2001), 35.

10. Timothy Cain, *The God of Great Reversals: The Gospel in the Book of Esther* (self-pub., 2016), 61.

11. Brueggemann, *Prophetic Imagination*, 12.

12. Brueggemann, *Prophetic Imagination*, 57.

13. "Do nothing out of selfish ambition or vain conceit. Rather, in humility value others above yourselves, not looking to your own interests but each of you to the interests of the others" (Phil. 2:3–4).

14. Soong-Chan Rah, *Prophetic Lament: A Call for Justice in Troubled Times* (Downers Grove, IL: InterVarsity, 2015), 22.

15. Rah, *Prophetic Lament*, 58.

16. Rah, *Prophetic Lament*, 58.

17. Rah, *Prophetic Lament*, 72.
18. Brueggemann, *Prophetic Imagination*, 76.
19. Martin Luther King Jr., *Stride toward Freedom: The Montgomery Story* (Boston: Beacon, 2010), 39.
20. The Golden Rule is derived from Matthew 7:12.
21. McNeil, *Becoming Brave*, 142.
22. McNeil, 57.

Chapter 4: Moses

1. W. E. B. Du Bois, *The Souls of Black Folk* (Mineola, NY: Dover, 1994), 5.
2. Britt Evans, "The Other Pandemic: Unpacking the Mental and Physical Health Consequences of Racism," Chicago Psychotherapy, September 19, 2020, https://www.chicago -psychotherapy.com/cp-blog/2020/9/19/racism-is-a-pandemic.
3. Brenda Salter McNeil, *Roadmap to Reconciliation 2.0* (Downers Grove, IL: InterVarsity, 2015), 113.
4. Howard Thurman, *Deep Is the Hunger* (Chicago: Friends United, 1978), 9.
5. Bessel van der Kolk, *The Body Keeps the Score: Brain, Mind, and Body in the Healing of Trauma* (New York: Penguin Books, 2014), 3.
6. Van der Kolk, *The Body Keeps the Score*, 21.
7. Van der Kolk, *The Body Keeps the Score*, 42.
8. Justo L. González, *Santa Biblia: The Bible through Hispanic Eyes* (Nashville: Abingdon, 1996), 111–12.
9. Maya Angelou, "People Have to Develop Courage," Maya Angelou on the March on Washington 50th Anniversary, CNN, August 28, 2013, https://www.youtube.com /watch?v=UxkTd6BFL1o.
10. Martin Luther King Jr., "Letter from a Birmingham Jail," April 16, 1963.
11. King, "Letter from a Birmingham Jail."
12. W. E. B. Du Bois, *The Ordeal of Mansart: The Black Flame Trilogy: Book One* (Oxford: Oxford University Press, 2014), 275.

13. Quoted in Jerry Windley-Daoust, *Primary Source Readings in Catholic Social Justice* (Winona, MN: Saint Mary's Press, 2007), 35.

14. Willie James Jennings, "My Anger, God's Righteous Indignation / Willie Jennings (Response to the Death of George Floyd)," For the Life of the World, Yale Center for Faith and Culture, episode 13, June 2, 2020, https://for-the -life-of-the-world-yale-center-for-faith-culture.simplecast .com/episodes/my-anger-gods-righteous-indignation-willie -jennings-response-to-the-death-of-george-floyd-FXkkWh9b /transcript.

15. Martin Luther King Jr., "Loving Your Enemies," Sermon, Dexter Avenue Baptist Church, November 17, 1957, http://okra.stanford.edu/transcription/document _images/Vol04Scans/315_17-Nov-1957_Loving%20Your%20 Enemies.pdf.

16. Anne Ford, "A Church and Community Partnership Helps Bring Fresh Groceries to a Chicago Food Desert," Duke Divinity Faith and Leadership, February 19, 2019, https://faithandleadership .com/church-and-community-partnership-helps-bring-fresh -groceries-chicago-food-desert.

17. Jonathan Brooks, *Church Forsaken: Practicing Presence in Neglected Neighborhoods* (Downers Grove, IL: InterVarsity, 2018), 12.

18. Ford, "A Church and Community Partnership."

19. Ford, "A Church and Community Partnership."

Chapter 5: Paul and Silas

1. Bryan Stevenson, "Attorney Bryan Stevenson: Banning the Death Penalty Would 'Liberate Us,'" SuperSoul Sunday, interview with Oprah Winfrey, November 2, 2015, https://www .youtube.com/watch?v=ig8H7iatZpI.

2. Willie James Jennings, *Acts*, Belief: A Theological Commentary on the Bible (Louisville: Westminster John Knox, 2017), 165.

3. Jennings, *Acts*, 223.

4. Jennings, *Acts*, 165.

5. Jennings, *Acts*, 165.

6. Dominique DuBois Gilliard, "Bryan Stevenson Wants to Liberate People from the Lie That Their Life Doesn't Matter," *Christianity Today*, January 10, 2020, https://www .christianitytoday.com/ct/2020/january-web-only/just-mercy -film-bryan-stevenson.html.

7. Gilliard, "Bryan Stevenson Wants to Liberate People."

Chapter 6: Jesus

1. Michael J. Gorman, *Cruciformity: Paul's Narrative Spirituality of the Cross* (Grand Rapids: Eerdmans, 2001), 47.

2. Gorman, *Cruciformity*, 61.

3. Gorman, *Cruciformity*, 47.

4. Justo González, *Luke*, Belief: A Theological Commentary on the Bible (Louisville: Westminster John Knox, 2010), 56.

5. González, *Luke*, 57.

6. González, *Luke*, 59.

7. González, *Luke*, 56.

8. Esau McCaulley, *Reading While Black: African American Biblical Interpretation as an Exercise in Hope* (Downers Grove, IL: IVP Academic, 2020), 58.

9. The NAS New Testament Greek Lexicon, s.v., "Ptochos," Bible Study Tools, accessed September 28, 2020, https://www .biblestudytools.com/lexicons/greek/nas/ptochos.html#.

10. Bible Hub, s.v., "oppressed," accessed September 28, 2020, https://biblehub.com/topical/o/oppressed.htm.

11. Bible Study Tools, s.v., "Jubilee Year," accessed September 28, 2020, https://www.biblestudytools.com/dictionary/jubilee -year/.

12. Drew Hart, *Who Will Be a Witness? Igniting Activism for God's Justice, Love, and Deliverance* (Scottdale, PA: Herald, 2020), 85.

13. Howard Thurman, *Jesus and the Disinherited*, repr. ed. (Boston: Beacon, 1996), 1.

14. Matthew Heimer, "'Do Some Uncomfortable and Inconvenient Things': A Civil Rights Champion's Call to Action for CEOs," *Fortune*, June 26, 2018, https://fortune.com/2018/06/26/bryan -stevenson-ceo-initiative/.

15. González, *Luke*, 52.

Chapter 7: Zacchaeus

1. *The Uncomfortable Truth*, written and directed by Loki Mulholland (Taylor Street Films, 2017).

2. Zoe Thomas, "The Hidden Links between Slavery and Wall Street," *BBC*, August 28, 2019, https://www.bbc.com/news /business-49476247.

3. Ken Magill, "From J.P. Morgan Chase, an Apology and $5 Million in Slavery Reparations," *New York Sun*, February 1, 2005, https://www.nysun.com/business /from-jp-morgan-chase-an-apology-and-5-million/8580/.

4. Rachel L. Swarns, "Insurance Policies on Slaves: New York Life's Complicated Past," New York Times, December 18, 2016, https://www.nytimes.com/2016/12/18/us/insurance -policies-on-slaves-new-york-lifes-complicated-past.html.

5. Sven Beckert and Seth Rockman, eds., *Slavery's Capitalism: A New History of American Economic Development*, Early American Studies (Philadelphia: University of Pennsylvania Press, 2016), 3.

6. Nikole Hannah-Jones, "The Economy That Slavery Built," interview with Matthew Desmond, *New York Times*, 1619 Podcast, episode 2, https://www.nytimes .com/2019/08/30/podcasts/1619-slavery-cotton-capitalism .html.

7. David W. Blight, "The Civil War and Reconstruction Era, 1845–1877," Open Yale Courses, course no. HIST 119.

8. Elsa Tamez, *Bible of the Oppressed* (Maryknoll, NY: Orbis, 2007), 22.

9. Pheme Perkins, "Taxes in the New Testament," *Journal of*

Religious Ethics 12, no. 2 (Fall 1984): 182, www.jstor.org/stable
/40014983.

10. Perkins, "Taxes in the New Testament," 183.

11. Perkins, "Taxes in the New Testament," 183.

12. M. I. Finley, *The Ancient Economy*, vol. 43 (Berkeley: University
of California Press, 1999), 90.

13. Adolf Hausrath, *A History of the New Testament Times: The Time
of Jesus*, vol. 1, trans. Charles T. Poynting and Philip Quenzer
(Norderstedt, Germany: Hansebooks, 2020), 188.

14. Hausrath, *A History of the New Testament Times*, 188.

15. Merrill C. Tenney, ed., *The Zondervan Pictorial Bible Dictionary*
(Grand Rapids: Zondervan, 1967), 598.

16. Alan D. Campbell, "Monetary System, Taxation, and Publicans
in the Time of Christ," *Accounting Historians Journal* 13, no.
2 (1986): 133, https://egrove.olemiss.edu/cgi/viewcontent
.cgi?article=1276&context=aah_journal.

17. Naphtali Lewis, *Life in Egypt under Roman Rule* (Oxford:
Clarendon, 1983), 165–66.

18. Tenney, *Zondervan Pictorial Bible Dictionary*, 828.

19. Lewis A. Muirhead, *The Times of Christ* (Sydney: Wentworth,
2019), 36.

20. Joseph Fitzmyer, *The Gospel according to Luke* (New York:
Doubleday, 1982), 469–70.

21. Justo González, *Luke*, Belief: A Theological Commentary on the
Bible (Louisville: Westminster John Knox, 2010), 222.

22. Campbell, "Monetary System, Taxation, and Publicans," 134.

23. Tamez, *Bible of the Oppressed*, 78.

24. Dennis Hamm, "Zacchaeus Revisited Once More: A Story
of Vindication or Conversion?" *Biblica* 72, no. 2 (1991): 252,
http://www.jstor.org/stable/42611178.

25. González, *Luke*, 220.

26. *An Unlikely Friendship*, directed by Diane Bloom, PBS, season
2019, episode 4.

27. *An Unlikely Friendship*.

28. *An Unlikely Friendship.*

29. Bryan Stevenson, "Love Is the Motive," On Being with Krista Tippett, December 3, 2020, https://onbeing.org/programs /bryan-stevenson-love-is-the-motive/#transcript.

30. Mike Fannin, "The Truth in Black and White: An Apology from *The Kansas City Star*," December 20, 2020, https: //www.kansascity.com/news/local/article247928045 .html?fbclid=IwAR2peDO5b-13VUSeyHHeiLiSUMNN6Wk8lNR lZDbo40NLD6sRDtXyGobEEfI.

31. Fannin, "The Truth in Black and White."

32. Fannin, "The Truth in Black and White."

33. Fannin, "The Truth in Black and White."

34. Fannin, "The Truth in Black and White."

35. Rachel L. Swarns, "Is Georgetown's $400,000-a-Year Plan to Aid Slave Descendants Enough?" *New York Times*, October 30, 2019, https://www.nytimes.com/2019/10/30/us/georgetown-slavery -reparations.html.

36. Terra Brockman, "A Church Returns Land to American Indians," *Christian Century*, March 3, 2020, https://www.christiancentury.org/article/features/church -returns-land-american-indians.

37. Brockman, "A Church Returns Land."

38. Brockman, "A Church Returns Land."

39. Brockman, "A Church Returns Land."

40. Brockman, "A Church Returns Land."

41. "Burge Resolution," City of Chicago, https://www.chicago.gov /content/dam/city/depts/dol/supp_info/Burge-Reparations -Information-Center/BurgeRESOLUTION.pdf.

42. "The Reparations Ordinance," Chicago Torture and Justice Memorials, January 17, 2020, https://chicagotorture.org /reparations/ordinance/.

43. "Burge Resolution," City of Chicago.

44. Jason Meisner, "City Agrees to Pay $9.3 Million for Wrongful Conviction Tied to Burge Detectives," *Chicago Tribune*, January

10, 2018, https://www.chicagotribune.com/news/breaking/ct
-met-wrongful-conviction-jon-burge-20180110-story.html.

Chapter 8: Scripture's Call to Repentance

1. Martin Luther King Jr., "Letter from a Birmingham Jail," April 16, 1963.
2. "Statement by Alabama Clergymen," Estate of Martin Luther King Jr., April 6, 1963, https://kinginstitute.stanford.edu/sites /mlk/files/lesson-activities/clergybirmingham1963.pdf.
3. "Reconstruction in America: Racial Violence after the Civil War, 1865–1876," Equal Justice Initiative, 6–7, accessed January 20, 2021, https://eji.org/wp-content/uploads/2020/07 /reconstruction-in-america-report.pdf.
4. Michael J. Perry, *Human Rights in the Constitutional Law of the United States* (Cambridge: Cambridge University Press, 2013), 9.
5. *The Uncomfortable Truth*, written and directed by Loki Mulholland (Taylor Street Films, 2017).
6. "Reconstruction in America," 6–7.
7. *Uncomfortable Truth.*
8. Stewart Emory Tolnay and E. M. Beck, *A Festival of Violence: An Analysis of Southern Lynchings, 1882–1930* (Champaign: University of Illinois Press, 1995), 28.
9. James Cone, *The Cross and the Lynching Tree* (New York: Orbis, 2011), 7.
10. Rian Dundon, "Photos: Less Than a Century Ago, 20,000 People Traveled to Kentucky to See a White Woman Hang a Black Man," Timeline, February 23, 2018, https://timeline.com/rainy-bethea -last-public-execution-in-america-lischia-edwards-6f035f61c229.
11. Orville D Menard, "Lest We Forget: The Lynching of Will Brown, Omaha's 1919 Race Riot,"
12. *Nebraska History* 91 (2010): 152–65, https://history.nebraska .gov/sites/history.nebraska.gov/files/doc/publications /NH2010Lynching.pdf.
13. Kurt Terry, "Jesse Washington Lynching," *Waco History*,

accessed January 20, 2021, https://wacohistory.org
/items/show/55.

14. "Duluth Lynchings: Resources Relating to the Tragic Events of
June 15, 1920," Minnesota Historical Society, accessed January
20, 2021, https://www.mnhs.org/duluthlynchings/.

15. "Public Spectacle Lynchings," Equal Justice Initiative,
accessed January 20, 2021, https://eji.org/news/history
-racial-injustice-public-spectacle-lynchings/.

16. Robert Moats Miller, "The Protestant Churches and Lynching,
1919–1939," *Journal of Negro History* 42, no. 2 (1957): 118, www
.jstor.org/stable/2715687.

17. The father and son have been indicted for murder and
aggravated assault, and their neighbor for felony murder and
criminal attempt to commit false imprisonment.

18. Robert J. Schroeder, "Memorandum: Louisville Metro
Police Department," letter to Detective Brent Hankison
#6150 Criminal Interdiction Division, June 19, 2020, https:
//interactive.whas11.com/pdf/HankisonTermination.pdf.

19. Isabel Wilkerson, *Caste: The Origins of Our Discontents* (New
York: Penguin Random House, 2020), 15.

20. Óscar A. Romero, *The Violence of Love* (Maryknoll, NY: Orbis,
2004), 30.

21. Esau McCaulley, *Reading While Black: African American Biblical
Interpretation as an Exercise in Hope* (Downers Grove, IL: IVP
Academic, 2020), 31. Italics in original.

22. McCaulley, *Reading While Black*, 34.

23. McCaulley, *Reading While Black*, 35.

24. McCaulley, *Reading While Black*, 39.

25. McCaulley, *Reading While Black*, 39.

26. King, "Letter from a Birmingham Jail."

27. King, "Letter from a Birmingham Jail."

28. King, "Letter from a Birmingham Jail."

29. Martin Luther King Jr., *A Knock at Midnight* (New York: Warner,
2000), 73.

30. Rashawn Ray, "How We Rise: Five Things John Lewis Taught Us about Getting in 'Good Trouble,'" Brookings, July 23, 2020, https://www.brookings.edu/blog/how-we-rise/2020/07/23/five-things-john-lewis-taught-us-about-getting-in-good-trouble/.

Chapter 9: Producing Fruit in Keeping with Repentance

1. Isabel Wilkerson, *Caste: The Origins of Our Discontents* (New York: Penguin Random House, 2020), 13.

2. Matthew Soerens and Jenny Yang, *Welcoming the Stranger: Justice, Compassion, and Truth in the Immigration Debate*, rev. and exp. ed. (Downers Grove, IL: InterVarsity, 2018), 86.

3. Soerens and Yang, 92.

4. "Evangelical Views on Immigration," Lifeway Research, February 2015, http://lifewayresearch.com/wp-content/uploads/2015/03/Evangelical-Views-on-Immigration-Report.pdf.

5. Robert Chao Romero, *Brown Church: Five Centuries of Latina/o Social Justice, Theology, and Identity* (Downers Grove, IL: InterVarsity, 2020), 38.

6. René Padilla, *The Local Church, Agent of Transformation: An Ecclesiology for Integral Mission* (Buenos Aires: Kairos Ediciones, 2004), 9.

7. Willie James Jennings, *Acts*, Belief: A Theological Commentary on the Bible (Louisville: Westminster John Knox, 2017), 223.

8. Jennings, *Acts*, 224.

9. Jennings, *Acts*, 225.

10. Jennings, *Acts*, 225.

11. Dominique DuBois Gilliard, "Bryan Stevenson Wants to Liberate People from the Lie That Their Life Doesn't Matter," *CT*, January 10, 2020, https://www.christianitytoday.com/ct/2020/january-web-only/just-mercy-film-bryan-stevenson.html.

12. "Bryan Stevenson Urges Campus to Get 'Proximate' on Issues of Race and Injustice," Texas Lutheran University, February 23, 2016, http://legacy.tlu.edu/blog/bryan-stevenson-urges-campus-to-get-proximate-on-issues-of-race-and-injusti/.

13. Bryan Stevenson, "4 Rules for Achieving Peace and Justice," Harvard Kennedy School, January 31, 2019, https://www .youtube.com/watch?v=9vI7UPuCUrE.

14. Walter Brueggemann, *Using God's Resources Wisely: Isaiah and Urban Possibility* (Louisville: Westminster John Knox, 1993), 64.

15. Donald Gowan, "Wealth and Poverty in the Old Testament: The Case of the Widow, the Orphan, and the Sojourner," *Interpretation: A Journal of Bible and Theology* 41, no. 4 (October 1987): 341.

16. Brueggemann, *Using God's Resources Wisely*, 66.

17. Wendell Berry, *The Hidden Wound*, 2nd ed. (Berkeley: Counterpoint, 2010), 129.

18. Drew Hart, *Who Will Be a Witness? Igniting Activism for God's Justice, Love, and Deliverance* (Scottdale, PA: Herald, 2020), 34.

19. Martin Luther King Jr., National Radio Project, at Brown Chapel, May 31, 1965, https://www.radioproject.org /transcript/2000/0039.html.

20. Chanequa Walker-Barnes, *I Bring the Voices of My People: A Womanist Vision for Racial Reconciliation* (Grand Rapids: Eerdmans, 2019), 70.

21. Dan Cathy, Lecrae, Louie Giglio, "The Beloved Community," Passion City Church, June 15, 2020, https://passion-city -church-podcast.simplecast.com/episodes/the -beloved-community-dan-cathy-lecrae-louie-giglio-BsHkD_gG.

22. Cathy, Lecrae, Giglio, "Beloved Community."

23. Richard A. Villodas Jr., Facebook, June 16, 2020, https://www.facebook.com/1659581615/posts /10220761184533683/?extid=KYmkzmpfBw4KsaoJ&d=n.

24. Villodas, Facebook.